Invitation to the Feast

DANNY E. BUSH

INVITATION TO THE FEAST

BROADMAN PRESS
Nashville, Tennessee

Unless otherwise indicated, all Scriptures are from the King James Version of the Bible. All marked RSV are from the Revised Standard Version of the Bible, copyrighted 1946, 1952, © 1971, 1973.; all marked Phillips are reprinted with permission of Macmillan Publishing, Inc. from J. B. Phillips: *The New Testament in Modern English,* Revised Edition. © J. B. Phillips 1958, 1960, 1972.; all marked GNB are from the *Good News Bible,* the Bible in Today's English Version, New Testament: Copyright © American Bible Society 1966, 1971, 1976. Used by permission.; all marked Williams are from *The New Testament, a Translation in the Language of the People,* by Charles B. Williams, Copyright 1937 and 1966, Moody Press, Moody Bible Institute of Chicago. Used by permission.

Library of Congress Cataloging-in-Publication Data

Bush, Danny E., 1939-
  Invitation to the feast.

  1. Baptists—Sermons.   2. Sermons, American.
3. Jesus Christ—Significance—Sermons.   I. Title.
BX6333.B87I58   1985   242   85-13314
ISBN 0-8054-5019-X (pbk.)

Contents

Foreword

The inevitability of this book has been clear to me from the beginning of a friendship with the author. As a matter of fact, Danny Bush's incredible energy and enthusiasm have found expression in *Invitation to the Feast*. I am personally grateful that his talent has come to fruition in this manner.

These thoughts come from an unusual mind, and they will indeed become food for the soul. The author sees things from an equally unusual perspective. This is not your usual fare. Neither is it a rearrangement of the same devotional material we "cut our teeth on."

What I like most about the content is: it is written for those of us who are neither spiritual idiots nor advanced theologians—just ordinary people with a little knowledge who hunger and thirst after rightesouness.

—CARL E. BATES
Louisville, Kentucky

About the Author

Rev. Danny E. Bush is associate minister-minister of education at First Baptist Church, Oak Ridge, Tennessee. Since 1961 he has served churches as minister of music, education, youth, and/or associate pastor in Tennessee, North Carolina, Maryland, Texas, and Virginia.

His writing includes training aids, devotional articles, puppet plays, sermons, essays, and Bible study materials. He has degrees from Belmont College and Southwestern Baptist Theological Seminary and has done other study at Southern Baptist Theological Seminary, Furman University, and the University of North Carolina at Charlotte. He has written for *Home Bible Study Guide*, *Adult Training Guide*, *Church Training*, *Skill for Leaders*, *The Deacon*, and *Sunday School Leadership*, ministers' manuals, and denominational papers.

Preface

A recent advertisement went, "Soup is good food." True. However, a steady diet of soup alone would soon prove boring and even insufficient. The same concept could be applied to the church, Christianity, or you as an individual Christian.

Dr. Foy Valentine, executive director of the Christian Life Commission of the Southern Baptist Convention, told our congregation that our denomination has rightfully placed emphasis on the security of believers and now must move to an equal emphasis on works, the application of our faith.

My mentor, Dr. Carl Bates, senior professor of preaching at Southern Baptist Theological Seminary, and I share a conviction that Christians can handle a far broader and more comprehensive diet of truth more often than thought possible.

I am indebted to my Christian parents who have always encouraged me to think, as well as act; college and seminary professors who spoke up to me and not down; church teachers and preachers who nourished my faith from childhood; my wife, Nadine, who has encouraged me, offering constructive ideas for the writing of this book; but most of all, the patience of Almighty God who urges His followers to act lovingly, creatively, and aggressively.

My prayer is that the readers of this book will be enriched in their Christian faith and challenged to nobler deeds to fellow humankind in the name of Christ.

DANNY E. BUSH
Oak Ridge, TN

Invitation to the Feast

1
Jesus,
the Life of the Party

Wedding receptions are joyous occasions. Sometimes there is more food than punch, cake, and mints. Often there are enough hors d'oeuvres, dip, and ham biscuits to make a hearty meal.

At these festive times the food is rich, and the air itself seems electrified with enthusiasm and happiness. The bride is beautiful, the groom is handsome, and the wedding party is dashing. Familiar odors from warm candle wax, floral arrangements, cake icing, and dry-cleaned, rental tuxedos mix to form a unique fragrance that will be remembered for years to come. Especially will this fragrance be recalled by the newlyweds and their parents. Even the last-minute replacement of the photographer who failed to show, the wedding ring the ring bearer dropped during the ceremony, and rice that keeps showing up in the honeymoon car a year after the wedding will all be remembered and cherished.

Gentiles in the twentieth century can put on quite a bash at a wedding party. But nothing we do begins to compare with the tremendous shindig a Jewish family could put together in the first century. At times the party would go for a week or more! To this day our Jewish friends continue to arrange a joyous time following marriages. The festivities do not last as long as did those of their forefathers, but the goings-on are merry, nonetheless.

In this atmosphere our Lord found Himself as recorded in the Gospel of John:

Two days later there was a wedding in the town of Cana in Galilee. Jesus' mother was there, and Jesus and his disciples had also been invited to the wedding. When the wine had given out, Jesus' mother said to him, "They are out of wine." "You must not tell me what to do," Jesus replied. "My time has not yet come." Jesus' mother then told the servants, "Do whatever he tells you." The Jews have rules about ritual washing, and for this purpose six stone water jars were there, each one large enough to hold between twenty and thirty gallons. Jesus said to the servants, "Fill these jars with water." They filled them to the brim, and then he told them, "Now draw some water out and take it to the man in charge of the feast." They took him the water, which now had turned into wine, and he tasted it. He did not know where this wine had come from (but, of course, the servants who had drawn out the water knew); so he called the bridegroom and said to him, "Everyone else serves the best wine first, and after the guests have drunk a lot, he serves the ordinary wine. But you have kept the best wine until now!" Jesus performed this first miracle in Cana in Galilee; there he revealed his glory, and his disciples believed in him (2:1-11, GNB).

Throughout our lives as the people of God there may be a tendency to vacillate between a pleasant, communicative posture and a pious aloofness. Put another way, Christians are the life of the party or they are more like "party poopers." One remark I have heard to describe a dull, lifeless individual is, "He is so down in the mouth that he could lap up a bowl of buttermilk with his lower lip without a spoon."

New Testament scholar William Barclay comments about our Lord at the wedding of Cana and then asks a pertinent question:

Jesus was perfectly at home at a wedding feast. He was no severe, austere killjoy. He loved to share in the happy rejoicing of a wedding feast. There are certain religious people who shed a gloom wherever they go. There are certain people who are suspicious of all joy and happiness. To them religion is the thing of the black clothes, the lowered voice, the expulsion of social fellowship. They descend like a gloom wher-

ever they go. . . . Jesus never counted it a crime to
be happy. Why should His followers do so?[1]

Of course, all of life for Christians or non-
Christians will not be bright like a fresh spring
day after a shower or colorful like a color-
drenched forest of trees in fall. The earthbound
life of Jesus was not always easy nor are our lives
today. Life was real then and now. Life was hard
then and now. Life was packed with a variety of
feelings and experiences then and now. But for
the Christian, whatever comes in life it is possible to avoid an attitude of final defeat. Why?
Because the more trust and belief you and I
place in Christ, the less we will be dependent on
religious traditions, possessions, popularity, or
whatever else.

Jesus determined always to please the Father and not man. This always proved the best
choice for Him. It is always our best choice to
seek pleasing the Heavenly Father and not mankind. Whether at a wedding feast in Cana or
from a cruel cross outside Jerusalem, Jesus was
victorious and pointed people to the works and
ways of the Father. He was literally the "life" of
the party, regardless of the circumstances.

John writes with enthusiasm about the Messiah. He uses much beautiful symbolism to express important concepts about the true

kingdom of God. James E. Carter invites Bible students to consider that, "In the Gospel of John the word *sign* is used rather than *miracle*. A sign points beyond itself to a major truth about God made known through Jesus Christ. A miracle is never a miracle for its own sake. As used by the writer of John's Gospel the miracle is always a sign that points beyond the event to a greater truth."[2]

Alert students of Jehovah God two thousand years ago and now must listen to the Word of God when it comes to them. Avoidance of preconceived notions about what God "ought to say" about a given matter will help us to catch what God is actually saying.

One contemporary teacher reminds us of something important about the writing style and points made in the teachings of John:

Here our problem is not a poverty of detail but an embarrassment of riches. As we shall often discover in the Johannine use of symbols, the evangelist shows many different facets of his theology through one narrative. Fortunately, the main import of the story is spelled out for us in vs. 11 . . . ("and his disciples believed in him.") . . . John does not put *primary* emphasis on the replacing of the water for Jewish purifications, nor on the action of changing water to wine (which is not described in detail), nor even on the resultant wine. John does not put primary emphasis on Mary or her intercession, nor on why she pursued her request, nor on the reaction of the head-waiter or of the groom. The primary focus is, as in all Johannine stories, on Jesus as the one sent by the Father to bring salvation to the world. What shines through is *his glory,* and the only reaction that is emphasized is the *belief* of the disciples."[3]

Reflect back on your experiences related to weddings. As a minister who has conducted wedding ceremonies in a variety of locations—churches, parks, private homes, church offices/studies—and as a guest viewing such ceremonies, I have observed the following:

1. The bride and groom evidently believe and trust in each other. This belief in each other has brought them to the point where they wish to share their lives together.

2. The wedding guests and visitors sense this belief the bride and groom have in each other. As the vows are exchanged, and the official celebration of partnership begins, there is an air of confidence that their mutual promises will be kept.

Just as Christian wedding vows are made before human witnesses and God, so are professions of faith in Christ made in the presence of a church fellowship and the Savior God. Decisions of such import should be made proudly in public. There is no shame in the marriage of two individuals or in the union of an individual with the Spirit of Christ.

A. M. Hunter offers some insight into the wedding story at Cana:

> Go back to Mark 2:19-22. There Jesus refers to himself and his disciples as a wedding party and speaks of the new wine of the kingdom of God bursting the old wine-skins of Judaism. This surely is the clue to the miracle's meaning. Jewish legalism, represented by the water of ritual purification, becomes the Gospel, the wine which gladdens the marriage-feast of the kingdom of God (Matt. 22:1-14). Judaism is water; Christianity is wine; and it is Christ who makes all the difference. For us today the lesson is not only that we must be transformed by Christ's power, but that it must happen not in a spirit of gloomy religiosity but in the context of joyous human fellowship.[4]

On Father's Day each year thousands of people express love and gratitude to living fathers or enjoy loving memories of fathers deceased. Our son was eight years of age when we adopted him back in the 1970s. He is as much our son as if he had been born to us like our daughter was in a neighborhood hospital. Our acceptance of one another as parents and child hinges largely upon our belief and trust in one another, not in blood relationship.

A marvelous fact of the child-Father relationship between a human believer and the

Heavenly Father is: the relationship is both one of adoption and bloodline, cleansing kinship. No more beautiful symbol can describe the intimate bond Christians have than that which the Son of God made possible at Calvary through the sacrificial shedding of His life-giving blood.

Symbolically speaking, Christians share in the spiritual wedding celebration because they are wedded to Jesus, "the life of the party." Each day we can say: This is the day which the Lord has made; let us rejoice and be glad in it. (Ps. 118:24, RSV).

2
Breakfast with the Christ

One of my favorite memories of my Grandaddy Lewis is winter breakfast with him at his old farmhouse in South Carolina. He would arise before the rest of us so he could gather fresh wood for the cookstove. After the stove was hot he would begin preparing the breakfast. The odor of the wood burning, coffee brewing, sausage frying in the pan, and biscuits baking would soon float in the air throughout the house. Those down-home fragrances were enough to awaken the soundest of sleepers.

Family members gathered quickly around the old stove in the country kitchen. Grandpa would pour coffee into his saucer so it would cool faster, blowing on it and then slurping it. Nobody seemed to mind the slurping. We were used to it and knew he was content and not likely to change.

There was always a variety of preserves to spread on the fresh, hot biscuits, or you could put fresh country butter and pour homemade molasses on the savory, steaming bread. My mouth waters even now just thinking about it. We were so cozy and satisfied. It was nothing elaborate, simply tasty, homemade country food—and lots of love. Come to think of it, there is practically nothing missing when the body is nourished with food and the soul is satisfied with love.

A tradition in my home, when I was young, was a big breakfast after attending the community Easter sunrise service. We would always have waffles and sausage instead of the usual cereal or eggs. This period of time was before nonstick waffle irons and spray-on vegetable oil. If done just right one could lift the hot waffles off the iron without too much sticking. Otherwise, one would have somewhat of a mess with part of the waffles stuck to the iron.

Sometimes your breakfast plate would have one almost-perfect waffle and mangled pieces. But it was such a treat with all that sweet syrup that we didn't mind. It was a joyous Christian day, we were together as a family, and there was plenty to eat. Those were so important. Later in the day we would visit relatives, have a big family picnic lunch, compare new Easter clothing and shoes, and hide Easter eggs in a pasture.

Arthur Pendenys was once quoted in the *New York Times:* "A good meal makes a man feel more charitable toward the whole world than any sermon."[1] Our Lord surely had this thought in mind as he prepared breakfast on the shore of the Sea of Tiberias. You can find and read the story of our Lord as breakfast chef recorded in John 21:1-14. He knew Peter, Thomas, Nathanael, James and John, the sons of Zebedee, and two unnamed disciples, had been fishing for a long time, and they were, no doubt, tired. After all, they had been out all night without catching a thing. They were hungry, weary, and confused. The Gospel writer relates that the risen Christ prepared breakfast for those tired fishermen. The thought is beautiful—the Son of God as a chef, a servant. Jesus was practicing what He taught and preached, "And whosoever will be chief among you, let him be your servant" (Matt. 20:27). Jesus was concerned with the physical needs of His followers then, and He is now. But spiritual matters are His primary concern.

John does not record any of the master's parables in his Gospel. He is eager for us to know who Jesus is and how faith in Him gives eternal life. This Gospel was written about AD 90. John reflects back on that breakfast he and six other disciples had with the Christ. So vivid an experience did John have that he even numbered how many fish were caught. After Jesus yelled to them, "Cast the net on the right side of the boat, and you will find some!" they obeyed, and those bone-weary men caught 153 fish!

Jesus had revealed Himself to the disciples before this breakfast appearance. Why were they somewhat confused and why were they back in the same old rut? In 21:12 John states that the disciples knew it was the Lord standing on the shore. And yet, they were doing the same old things.

We twentieth-century disciples must be kin to those early disciples. Even after Christ has revealed Himself to us we continue denying His power to make the situation different. Like those seven disciples of old we miss the point of what the kingdom of God is all about. Christians have gotten out of their beds many a morning, had breakfast, and then gone through the day with little or no follow-through in spreading the gospel, the good news. This is true, even though people who need the Bread of Life are all around Christians every day.

William Hull, in his commentary on the Gospel of John, wrote: "To Jesus, however, men were more than sheep or fish. To fish for fish is to take them from life into death, whereas to fish for men is to take them from death into life (cf. Mark 1:17)."[2]

Mark states that Jesus said to them: "Follow Me and I will make you become fishers of men" (Mark 1:17, NASB). "Come with me, and I will teach you to catch men" (Mark 1:17 GNB). When did Jesus speak these words to the disciples? He had given this same invitation to several of these same disciples by the same seashore about three years before this on-the-shore breakfast. And here they were putting the physical aspects of life ahead of spiritual. Does that behavior sound familiar?

I am not saying that Christ is not concerned with daily life after breakfast. Yes, He is aware of all our needs. It is not a matter of either physical needs or spiritual needs. This same Jesus who fellowships with us at the breakfast hours of life pleads with us to: "Instead, be concerned above everything else with the Kingdom of God and with what he requires of you, and he will provide you with all these other things" (Matt. 6:33, GNB).

As the Master Teacher, Jesus acted out a scene for the disciples similar to one they had experienced once before. Jesus served as a host at breakfast like he had at the Last Supper. At the Last Supper, Jesus served them bread and the fruit of the vine. Now at this breakfast Jesus prepared fish. He gave His body and blood so mankind could have eternal and abundant life. Jesus helped the disciples to tie those ideas together.

At the Passover meal with His disciples, directly before His death and resurrection, Jesus changed the meaning of that supper from a reminder of escape from slavery in a foreign land to a reminder of the sacrifice He made that brings freedom from the salvery of sin through faith in Him.

The Last Supper in the upper room had to come before breakfast on the seashore. It still does! Like children who want dessert in place of the main course, many Christian pilgrims want a calm, sweet life without ever coming to the main meat and potatoes of sacrifice and service. Getting a fresh start after breakfast is impossible if you have failed to partake from the supper of eternal life.

It is not surprising that to non-Christians or to uncommitted Christians, a person who is joyously serving Christ appears odd, out of step, even fanatical. Have you ever seen a young couple in love? To casual observers the behavior of the man and woman may appear strange. Sometimes they are oblivious to things happening all around them. At times they laugh when nothing seems to be funny.

If one has never been in love or fallen out of love one may have difficulty accepting people who are in love. A similar fact is true when practicing Christians are around non-Christians or spiritually cold Christians. The practicing Christians appear weird, different. People showing Christian love are strange people indeed to those whose hearts are filled with jealousy and hate.

Those early disciples on a fishing boat had for three years observed Christ's love in action, but they had not become vessels through whom love could flow. At this breakfast the Christ of Galilee would soon challenge them to follow Him in obedient service at all costs. Disciples centuries ago responded to the challenge of servanthood and left the seashore to become fishers of men. Many disciples today are responding to the challenge of servanthood, but multitudes more are needed!

In recent years the quiet but faithful service of a missionary in Calcutta, India, has come to the attention of the world. Mother Teresa was awarded the Nobel Peace Prize because of her unselfish ministry to the thousands of hungry, sick, and dying people of India. A while back I read her book entitled, *The Love of Christ,* a collection of spiritual counsels by this precious servant of the Lord. She is a contemporary example of a disciple who has experienced the love of Christ, is experiencing the love of Christ, and through whom the love of Christ is able to relieve human suffering. The following excerpts from that book offer excellent ideas about service for the Lord where one is.

> Do not imagine that love to be true must be extraordinary. No, what we need in our love is the continuity to love the One we love. See how a lamp burns, by the continual consumption of the little drops of oil. If there are no more of these drops in the lamp, there will be no light, and the Bridegroom has a right to say: "I do not know you."
>
> My children, what are these drops of oil in our lamps? They are the little things of everyday life: fidelity, punctuality, little words of kindness, just a little thought for others, those little acts of silence, of look and thought, of word and deed. These are the very drops of love that make our religious life burn with so much light.
>
> Do not search for Jesus in far off lands; He is not there. He is in you. Just keep the lamp burning and you will always see Him.[3]

Sometimes like the disciples of early New Testament days, we get the idea that service must always be "big," or it is insignificant. Granted, the followers of the Lord Christ should be people of vision. On the other hand we can just as easily fail to do anything by seeking only to do spectacular things.

The importance of doing little things came home to me in my experience during an airline flight. I had just finished a week of conducting an enlargement campaign in a Virginia church. It had been a great week. The Lord had blessed the church, the community, and my ministry marvelously. A hectic schedule including morning, afternoon, and evening activities left me refreshed but tired. On the plane I wanted to relax and not be such an "active" Christian.

A young couple with an infant were seated on the other side of the plane and down a few rows from me. They were such patient and loving parents. Caring for their fretful baby was a full-time occupation, and they were sharing the chores. I remember being a little weary of the child's disturbing noises.

Passengers in that high-flying metal bird were about to be served breakfast. The flight attendants were moving up and down the aisles serving the people. Near the end of the trip I began to be convicted. By the time I arrived home, my evaluation of how I behaved as a Christian troubled me. What I saw in myself was a facet of Christian life too often neglected in our teaching and preaching. It is also neglected in our home life many times. Practical, everyday Christian service is most often our chief opportunity for bearing a witness. On that airplane I had a chance to offer real assistance to two tired parents.

From an act of kindness I might have experienced the joy of sharing a personal testimony of my faith. If those parents were Christian they were a witness to me of the love and patience God can give mothers and fathers. Do you read me? After breakfast I could have been of service to someone. But, like those disciples on the seashore, I ate breakfast and was letting life go by. And the tired disciples were willing to eat breakfast and go on with "business as usual."

After breakfast Jesus challenged His disciples to "follow" Him. It is after breakfast now, symbolically speaking. Jesus is challenging all Christians to "follow" Him. Our discipleship is a moment-by-moment, hour-by-hour, day-by-day, and year-by-year process. We are to develop from weak or new servants to growing, productive saints in our own day.

A splendid Christian educator in our denomination, Dr. Harry Piland, says a church is in one of three categories—*decline, maintenance,* or *growth.* Numerical and spiritual growth are often obvious. Decline is also apparent. But maintenance is a condition that is often subtle. In a maintenance condition things don't seem to be too bad. In fact, things seem to be pretty good—no noticeable decline, smooth atmosphere. This is true of a church fellowship and an individual life. For certain, the maintenance condition cannot last forever—a church will eventually grow or decline. An individual life given to Christ cannot forever remain in a maintenance condition. Sooner or later that disciple will grow spiritually or grow colder or more indifferent. Is the oil in your Christian lamp glowing or flickering?

This year at a men's breakfast a dedicated man from another church spoke to our men about an effective mission-action program being conducted by his church, along with several other churches in his town. The program is a repairs or fix-it ministry for elderly or indigent people. He spoke of the real blessing to people in need being experienced through that Christian service. He also related how the participants were having their proverbial spiritual batteries recharged. Doors to witnessing in Christ's name can be opened as God's people live like Christians and serve like Christians.

There is another thought about lives given over to Christ. In their very nature and character, servants of the Lord have a glow of love. This glow is often obvious and most attractive. This truth came to me during my younger years and unforgettably blessed me.

In 1956 a group of older boys from North Carolina and South Carolina toured our denomination's mission work in Cuba. It was my privilege to be a part of that group. As a high school senior and child of parents who taught the values of personal initiative, I was not given money for the trip. Like the television commercial about an investment firm, "I had to earn it." Money for the trip was saved from earnings as a newspaper carrier in Charlotte, North Carolina, and summer commercial construction labor.

Be assured, that mission trip was earned and thoroughly enjoyed for many reasons. I can recall many experiences from that on-the-scene mission tour. One particularly meaningful event was a sunrise service and breakfast at an humble church retreat. We had to ride in an old bus to reach our place of retreat. The site was in the midst of thick jungle growth and wild animals. Our accommodations were extremely simple. We slept on old army bunks in fragile wood-frame buildings.

Following a time of becoming acquainted we all retired for the night. The sunrise service was scheduled for the next morning. As the sun rose we gathered on a clearing at the top of a mountain. I don't recall what the devotion was, who prayed, or what we sang, though we enjoyed all those. What I do recall is the deep Christian fellowship we had as American and Cuban Christians. My one year of high school Spanish helped some, but what we communicated was beyond any human language or speech pattern. It was spiritual kinfolk relating to one another. Like the early church, as recorded in the Acts of the Apostles, our love for one another in Christ was evident. It should be like that all the time.

Following the sunrise service in that tropical paradise we assembled in the dining hall for breakfast. Breakfast consisted of a mixture of half a cup of milk and half a cup of coffee, plus a big hunk of bread from a freshly baked common loaf. That was one of the most delicious breakfasts I have ever eaten. A vibrant sense of Christian love pervaded the air at that simple Cuban-American retreat. What a pity our nation foolishly let that lovely country fall into the hands of the Soviet Union. The Cubans are, by and large, such warm and friendly people, I have learned. We Christians in the United States need to pray for fellow Christians in Cuba, as well as for all Christians everywhere.

Breakfast with the Christ is always followed by the call to service, the call to live and proclaim His love. Our prayer could be:

Dear Bread of Heaven,

You have prepared a table before us. Feed us until we shall want no more.

Send us out to a hungry world to share the Bread of Life.

In the name of Jesus Christ, our loving Host, we pray.

Amen.

3
Dinner on the Grounds

At a family reunion or a church covered-dish dinner it is easy to overload your plate. The food usually spread out at these occasions is scrumptious. Most of the fare looks *good*. This wide assortment of food not only looks good and usually is, with an exception or two.

You know exactly what I mean when I say everything at a dinner on the grounds or covered-dish dinner appears delicious and hard to resist. That variety of meats, vegetables, breads, salads, and desserts challenges one to make the choice whether to gorge or to be selective.

I must confess, I have given in to overeating more often than to moderating my selections. For years I hid behind the excuse of piling my plate high with food because I did not want to offend any of the cooks in the congregation, or that it takes extra energy to be an active minister, so I had to eat plenty for the needed strength.

From previous experience I knew most of the food was luscious, and it was easier to let go than to moderate.

Something happens to your body when you pass forty years of age. Now that I am well past forty, my awareness of the change in my metabolism is greater. Instead of burning off many of the calories, my system has begun to retain those calories in the form of fat. For years I was blessed with a slender body. That slenderness still exists with one noticeable exception. Midway in my physique has appeared an expanded section. Some people humorously refer to this as "Donelaps disease." The abdominal region has "done lapped" over my waistband and belt. I've heard others comment, "I'm watching my weight. I'm letting it stick out where I can watch it." This watching technique is overdone when you can't see your feet while standing up or when it's necessary to wear slip-on shoes because it is impossible to bend over and tie your own shoes.

We can chuckle about this and go on with habits as they are, or honestly face the situation —and then take steps to avoid, and even put a stop to, things which contribute to overeating and overweight.

If we subscribe to the Scriptural injunction that one's "body is a temple of the Holy Spirit" (see 1 Cor. 3:16, author's words), then it follows that we should take care of the bodies which house the holy presence of the Lord. By this declaration of spiritual real estate I am not implying that mankind is the only residence of our Lord or that humans must be perfect abodes before the Holy Spirit will move in. Human perfection in itself is impossible.

Since God indwells the lives of those who invite him in, they need to take care of those mortal systems so they can be as fit as possible for service to the "Home Owner," God.

With this illustration of dinner on the grounds in mind—along with overeating and overdoing intake—think with me about the possibility of religion being "overdone."

At first you might be perplexed by this concept, especially when it is part of this book which emphasizes commitment and specific, practical application of Christian teachings. Like overeating can cause unusable fat and can ruin an otherwise trim body, so too much "religion" can adversely affect disciples and those whom they influence.

Added to the possibility of too much religion

are those times when a disciple gets involved in something beyond his/her maturity.

Early in my "professional" ministry I was invited by a rather large church to consider joining their staff as minister of youth. Naturally, I was excited and flattered by the opportunity. At that point in my Christian pilgrimage I had served on church staffs for several years. Those years of service had allowed me to direct the overall Christian education, youth, or music ministries in rural, city, and university city churches. So I was confident that I had matters well in hand; nothing was too good for me to tackle.

After mutual consideration the church felt led to look at other candidates. I was literally amazed at their seeming inability to recognize a "good thing" when they saw it. After being informed of their decision not to call me, my wife and I sat through their Sunday morning worship service. My indignation and pride kept me from enjoying a worship experience that day.

Years later, as I reflected on that experience, it became clear that, had I somehow been called to that position, most likely I would have made a total idiot of myself and would not have provided the right quality of leadership. The demands would have been too much for me for several reasons. One, apparently my motivation was self-centered—an ego trip—rather than an humble seeking of the Holy Spirit's leadership in my life. Two, even though I had several years of experience it was not enough of the kind needed to carry out the requirements of the position. Three, deep down I knew that concentrating on a vocation dealing primarily with teenagers was neither my calling nor my driving interest. Fortunately, God and the search committee knew all those reasons better than I.

Enthusiasm and sincerity for Christian service are desirable, but by themselves are not enough. It strikes me that in our churches we show signs, at times, of an epidemic. I refer to this epidemic as a "dinner-on-the-grounds" or "too-much-of-a-good-thing" syndrome. Many Christians assume that, since they have eaten sufficiently at the table of church attendance and activities, they are certainly well suited for whatever the church needs or calls on them to do. This assumption also affects marriage relationships, parent-child communication, and friendships. Church "busyness" simply cannot replace personal attention to day-to-day living out of the Christian ethic.

It is also possible for sincere followers of the Lord to assume that, because of their biblical-intellectual discipline (by way of personal study or academic pursuit), they are most adequately prepared for any dish the "kingdom kitchen" has to cook up and serve.

It is interesting how closely related are the biblical passages, 1 Kings 3:5-12, Matthew 13:44-52, and Romans 8:26-30. In them are certain vital ingredients for use in preparing and sustaining a sufficient, yet abundant, life. Blended, these ingredients are able to satisfy the most discerning spiritual diners.

Notice how Solomon sought what he needed for him to be leader of the chosen people. "And now, O Lord my God, thou hast made thy servant king in place of David my father, although I am but a little child; I do not know how to go out or come in" (1 Kings 3:7, RSV).

Theologian John Gray observes: "Hence his reference to himself as a 'little child' could be merely the conventional humility of prayer."[1]

Another writer says: "Measuring himself by the stature of his father, the young sovereign felt his littleness and his need. He became 'poor in spirit,' and poverty of spirit is the opposite of pride."[2]

Later in his rule Solomon strayed away from this childlike attitude toward serving the King of kings. At this early juncture he was definitely able to receive the direction and assignment God had for his life.

We are reminded of this childlike attitude

toward kingdom service in the New Testament: "Truly, I say to you, unless you turn and become like children you will never enter the kingdom of heaven" (Matt. 18:3, RSV).

A childlike attitude is necessary for one to be ushered by God into the dining hall of Christian living. It remains absolutely essential throughout every course in the feast of eternal life, prepared by the Lord, that we be like little children and eat only what is necessary under His direction.

Yes, we can gobble down everything within our reach only to experience proverbial "spiritual indigestion." The superior choice is to consume what is best for us at the direction of our devoted Father God.

Observe what Solomon prayed for God to give him to nourish his service as king. His request was not selfish. It was not a morsel of dessert to satisfy a whim. He asked for a blessing beyond himself and out of human grasp. Only the Creator could provide him the request. "Give thy servant therefore an understanding mind to govern thy people, that I may discern between good and evil; for who is able to govern this thy great people?" (1 Kings 3:9, RSV).

A Southern Baptist scholar, M. Pierce Matheny, in commenting on this passage, says:

An understanding mind to govern is literally "a hearing heart to judge," and refers to that practical wisdom required of the king as court of appeal for difficult cases such as the one that follows.[3]

Solomon felt that a king would need a profound commonsense skill in order to govern the people wisely, fairly, and insightfully.

A famous example of this wisdom follows in 1 Kings 3:16-28, where Solomon created a challenge to two women that resulted in the discovery of the real mother in a dispute over true maternity rights.

Productive Christian living today is a challenge, to say the least. In our pseudo-sophisticated ways it is easy for even the most sincere Christians to rely too much on their own ability, rather than on the work of God through them. We are conditioned in society to be self-sufficient. Leeches of society, whether their dependence be self-made or inherited, are looked on with reproach. These circumstances cause us to emphasize independence and self reliance. This seems good for a citizen of the world. For a citizen of the kingdom of God an attitude of dependency is a primary ingredient at all points of servanthood.

Speaking of the request by Solomon for wisdom, one says, "His prayer is worth frequent repetition as we face the continually changing problems of personal relationships in our own lives."[4]

It is important to clarify a point right here. You and I are profoundly dependent on God for everything. However, this does not mean that when we decide to take up our crosses and follow Christ we are to divorce ourselves from our God-given skills and cease from investing these gifts in satisfying ways.

It is quite the opposite. Whatever your gifts or mine, when they are placed at the disposal of the Lord God, we will derive far more than if we go it on our own. As William Barclay aptly comments on Matthew 13:51-52:

> Jesus did not come to empty life, but to fill it, not to impoverish life, but to enrich it. Here we see Jesus telling men, not to abandon their gifts, but to use them even more wonderfully because they are using them in the light of the knowledge which He has given them.[5]

The emptying of self allows room for the filling of the Spirit of God. God does not force Himself on people. We who follow Christ as our example should not allow ourselves to be bloated with self-overindulgence in religion and then throw our weight around. The feast of Christ is not ours to serve—it is His to serve through us. In this distinction we are prone to err.

The apostle Paul instructs the church at Rome and all who read the Word that there are times when the believer does not even know what to pray for (Rom. 8:26-30). Yet we are told in another instruction to "pray constantly" (1 Thess. 5:17). Is there a contradiction in these two teachings? No. Our minusucle view of the kingdom of God prevents us from knowing all that God is doing at any given time. We "see in a mirror dimly" (1 Cor. 13:12, RSV). "If the Spirit indwells the Christian, and that has been the chapter's (Romans 3) insistent theme, then God's mind mingles with ours in our prayers."[6]

Abraham Lincoln is quoted as testifying:

> I have been driven many times to my knees by the overwhelming conviction that I had nowhere else to go. My own wisdom, and that of all about me, seemed insufficient for the day.[7]

Many probably most often miss out on the feast of God by not understanding the nature of the kingdom of which we are part. Several biblical passages help us understand some concepts concerning the Kingdom of God—Matthew

13:44-52; Romans 1; Ephesians 2:8; and Revelation. These concepts, as I see them, are:

1. There is no price too great to pay for the kingdom of God.
2. It is a privilege to pay the price.
3. The net of God as He searches for the "fish" for his kingdom shows no preferences. Neither should we "caught" fish show preferences in our fishing.
4. We respond voluntarily to the truth of God as revealed to us.
5. The final judge in all aspects of the kingdom is God, not us. He is the judge of those who are part of his kingdom. He is the judge of the use of gifts by those in that kingdom.

The kingdom of God is far more than we can comprehend. It is wise for disciples to enjoy the spiritual food provided—Bible study, experiences of faith in action, counsel of mature Christians, corporate and private worship, and prayer. It is equally wise to avoid thinking we are overfed and fully adequate to be part of the Kingdom, no matter how good or faithful we think we are. The lesson of humility must be learned daily by well-known and not so well-known Christians.

Dear Father,

Deliver me from feelings of being well fed and
    a self-sufficient diner in your kingdom.
Instill within me the joy of your salvation.
Now that I am more aware of whose kingdom
    I am a part of
Nurture me daily by your divine presence,
    wisdom, and love.
Enter my every thought and deed that I may
    more perfectly feed others the truths of your
    holy kingdom.
Return, Lord Jesus, as you have promised,
    and may you find me and all your servants
    waiting in humble, obedient living and service.
    Amen.

4
The Tacos Fold

The first time I ate a taco I couldn't imagine food like that—a stiff pad of corn dough with assorted vegetables and meat thrown in—being worth much. To my pleasant surprise, tacos are delicious! Besides that they provide quick food without much fuss. Tacos are convenient. Tacos are simple. Tacos may hardly compare with steak and all the trimmings, but they are food.

Our food in America is designed for convenience. That is a main reason why so many fast-food restaurants keep popping up everywhere in our land. Whether in large cities or small towns you will notice an assortment of convenience-type restaurants pushing hamburgers, fried chicken, deli sandwiches, steaks, and tacos.

Convenience is a by-product of American life. We want clothes washing convenient so we install washers and dryers in our homes or apartments. To make receiving or dialing telephone calls convenient, many people have more than one telephone installed—or have one of those new cordless models so they can carry it around the house or out in the yard.

The philosophy, "I want what I want when I want it," is the theme of our contemporary society. An extension of this philosophy is, "I will do what I want to do when I want to do it." Convenience is our way of thinking and living.

Convenience to be and convenience to do as we will is a common human trait, especially in modern society. This attitude directly affects thousands of individuals, families, communities, and nations. Consequently, this attitude disrupts otherwise happy and contented people. Ask any labor-relations officer, policeman, businessman, school official, counselor, or minister how the attitude of "doing what I want" affects society, and you will probably hear groaning, then affirmation that it is a root cause of most behavioral problems.

Somewhere you may have seen or heard "SIN" illustrated as: "I" is the center of a life without Christ, so *sin* prevails.

A preference for few, if any, attachments and obligations is desired by most people. One

extreme of this "taco" life-style is a bum, a vagabond, a floater.

Another category of the "taco" life-style is
composed of those persons who take on barely
enough responsibility to satisfy a limited number
of rules or requirements.

Most persons in this last group may resist
being compared to the vagabond. But in actual-
ity their "taco"-type existence produces a similar
end and a similar output. Their philosophy is to
get by scarcely. This approach to life makes their
output meager or almost nothing.

The drifter lives a hand-to-mouth existence
on a disorganized schedule from town to town.
He "gets by." There are few or no attachments
for the bum. He lives a "taco" life-style. This
life-style I classify as "taco" living, quick, without
much fuss, low cost, convenient. This life-style is
kind of like that of a sophisticated vagabond.

Our churches are filled with members who
either seldom attend or have the impression
that, if they attend revival services, go on a choir
tour, give a "fair" share of money, don't beat
their wives, husbands, or kids, or kick their dogs,
their obligations to Christ are pretty well satisfied.

Recently I read a remarkable story about a
man who was almost killed by three 7,200-volt
blasts of electricity. For three and a half hours he

was presumed dead. Over 80 percent of his body was burned; his skull was so badly burned that doctors had to replace part of it with a plastic plate. He spent nearly a year in the hospital and had to learn to walk again.

This Christian man has testified he is not bitter about the accident. He thanks God for the strength to survive it. In a small book he describes his ordeal and victory over it. In an interview he commented, "I know blind and handicapped people who can do amazing things. Then I've seen people who I totally believe could get up and move a little bit more if they put out the effort. That's what this book is about. I believe in survivors."[1]

Figuratively speaking, the man in this newspaper story prefers more than a "taco" existence which is convenient, painless, and a means of just getting by.

The beautiful story of Stephen as recorded by Luke is about tragedy and victory. In picturesque language that reveals the nuances of the Greek, J. B. Phillips translates Acts 7:51-60 as follows:

"You obstinate people, heathen in your thinking, heathen in the way you are listening to me now! It is always the same—you never fail to resist the Holy Spirit! Just as your fathers did, so are you doing now.

Can you name a single prophet whom your fathers did not persecute? They killed the men who long ago foretold the coming of the just one, and now in our own day you have become his betrayers and his murderers. You are the men who have received the law of God miraculously, by the hand of the angels, and you are the men who have disobeyed it!"

These words stung them to fury and they ground their teeth at him in rage. Stephen, filled through all his being with the Holy Spirit, looked steadily up into Heaven. He saw the glory of God, and Jesus himself standing at his right hand.

"Look!" he exclaimed, "the heavens are opened and I can see the Son of Man standing at God's right hand!"

At this they put their fingers in their ears. Yelling with fury, as one man they made a rush at him and hustled him out of the city and stoned him. The witnesses of the execution flung their clothes at the feet of a young man by the name of Saul.

So they stoned Stephen while he called upon God, and said, "Jesus, Lord, receive my spirit!" Then, on his knees, he cried in ringing tones, "Lord, forgive them for this sin." And with these words he fell into the sleep of death, while Saul gave silent assent to his execution.

It seems clear that Stephen would not be classified as a "taco" Christian. His courageous stand for the proclamation of the Messiah before (note this) religious people was not at all convenient or popular.

The commitment of Stephen had its costs. His sterling commitment cost the life of a child of God at the hands of religious, church-type people. One scholar commenting on this Scripture has written:

> The Jews had let their devotion to a *house* of worship take the place of loyalty to God. Throughout Christian history men have tended to deify buildings and sanctify places. Fellowship often is broken by a proposal to move the church *location* or to modify or replace the physical *facility*. "God is a spirit" and he dwells not in houses of wood but in the hearts of men and in the body of the believers which is the true church.
>
> The first Christian martyr was a layman! Stephen's death did not destroy his witness. The centuries to follow reveal that "the blood of martyrs is the seed of the church."[2]

For Stephen the presence and power of the Holy Spirit were sufficient for him to take a stand. It would have been far more convenient and easy for Stephen to stay at home that day almost two thousand years ago. But, no, he had to become involved. He went where the Spirit of God led him. Stephen had the concept that buildings were not the temples of God and that the lives of believers are the buildings for the kingdom of God. He believed his priority as a believer in the true Messiah was to live and to proclaim Jesus unashamedly, whatever the cost.

The late L. D. Johnson, former pastor and Furman University chaplain, relates this story as told by missionary E. Stanley Jones:

"A young man was arrested for preaching the kingdom of God," wrote E. Stanley Jones of India. When the fellow defended himself that he was preaching only what Jesus had preached long ago, the prosecutor argued, "But the Kingdom of God has not come yet." "It has for me," the young man replied.[3]

Most disciples of Christ are not called on to die physically for their faith. We are called on to possess the attitude or willingness to be martyrs for the faith, should it be necessary. If we are not careful we Christians will contribute to the suspicion of Christianity. Any cause for which its advocates are unwilling to struggle becomes suspect, unimportant, and dies, or becomes so dormant it is ignored.

Once a school teacher became caught up in the great freedom movement of a band of people. He volunteered to be a spy behind enemy lines. His presence and purpose were discovered. Just before his execution by the enemy he uttered the following words which have become famous: "I only regret that I have but one life to give for my country." Nathan Hale was not a "taco" American. His service to the cause of freedom required a willingness to give everything, even his life.

Stephen the Christian martyr and Hale the patriot martyr had at least one thing in common.

They believed in what they stood for. Their motivation was not based on, "I'll take a stand if it is convenient." Their motivation was based on, "Here am I, send me."

Today, as never before, the cause of Christ needs people like Stephen and Hale. Stephen and Hale became famous for the roles they played in significant causes. But there have been countless unnamed thousands with similar courage and faith who have fought or died for Christ or their country. Their efforts were not in vain and were equally heroic and humble.

Generations of humanity are benefactors of those in the past who were willing to base their commitment on conviction and not convenience. Tacos fold, but a feast is spread with an abundance so many others can partake and can enjoy.

The gospel is a feast that can eternally nourish those who receive it in faith and commitment. To spread such a feast is not always convenient.

Those who spread the gospel feast are required to "pray without ceasing," to "take up" their "crosses daily," to keep on preaching-teaching, and to trust God, not self, programs, or denominations, for the results.

The gospel feast is spread by those disciples who avoid "taco" or convenient service.

5
The Three-Cent Half-Pint of Milk

My sister and I were reared in the city. Our family was included in that large sector of society called middle class. We were not rich by any means, but we did not have to do without. Because my sister and I were raised to appreciate initiative, it was our nature to show our parents we could do things on our own from time to time. During my elementary days in school I learned many foundational lessons.

One reality of life that came to me was: there really are poor people around us. The term "poor people" up to that point in life was somewhat vague and had to do with faulty ideas like: "Many people are lazy and don't work, so they are poor." "Some are from a long line of down-and-out people, so not much is expected of them." "It is generous and right for fortunate church people to help poor people at Thanksgiving and Christmas." With this in mind it is no surprise that my first genuine contact with a poor person was a shock, as well as a learning experience.

At school the cafeteria manager would give you a half-pint of milk free if you carried out the kitchen garbage can. My friend Tom had been doing this job before I came to his school. I knew Dad would be proud of me, so as often as possible I would get to the manager ahead of Tom, carry out the trash, and receive the milk award. Not only would Dad be proud of me for showing initiative, but I could also save the three cents to spend at the drug store or dime store on the way home from school.

One day Tom pushed me aside and hit me. His actions surprised me. My parents had always taught me not to fight, and besides that, the boy who had just struck me was a buddy. You don't get into fights with a buddy if you can help it. After Tom took the trash out he returned to the cafeteria to receive his free milk award.

The next day Tom and I had a talk about his behavior toward me. He told me his parents didn't have much money. The scales of ignorance began falling from my mind's eyes, and for the first time I truly saw Tom in clothes not as nice as mine and without the same kind of financial resources to which I was accustomed. Taking the trash cans out in return for free milk was important to both Tom and me—for different reasons. For me it was a way to make my father proud of me. For Tom it was survival.

Most of the people reading this book can go to their refrigerators and find something to eat. If the food assortment there is not exactly what the taste buds are longing for, a quick trip to the store can solve the problem. Because of this ready access to food it is sometimes difficult for the average American to visualize or fully understand the presence of hungry people in this country and starvation conditions around the world.

A few years ago Arthur Simon, executive director of Bread for the World, wrote a book with the same title as his organization. Sobering sentences open the first chapter entitled "Hunger":

> Hunger is a child with shriveled limbs and a swollen belly. It is the grief of parents, or a person gone blind for lack of vitamin A. A single example of hunger is one too many. But in 1974 the United Nations reported that by the most conservative estimate, more than 460 million people are permanently hungry. They don't get enough calories to make a normal life possible and their number is increasing. Without enough calories the body slows down and at

some point starts to devour its own vital proteins for energy.[1]

Not far from the sophisticated scientific research center of Oak Ridge, Tennessee, are hundreds of people living in the poverty of Appalachia. Some of the citizens of the well-fed city are aware of the plight of their neighbors close by. But because of affluence that tends to insulate the haves from the have nots, busy schedules, and a measure of indifference, many citizens remain ignorant of the realities of human need. This story is repeated all across this country, the land of the free and the brave that flows with milk and honey.

One good example of light where there is darkness, or food where there is hunger, is found in the response to need shown by members of First Baptist Church in Oak Ridge. A center was opened at the church to dispense clothing and food. Before it was opened, thorough preparation was made to provide suitable space, a sufficient volunteer staff on a regular schedule, church approval and backing, and, of course, food and clothing. The word spread around the area, and within a few months hundreds of genuinely needy people began to flock to the church for aid. Controls are maintained so as many individuals or families as possible can be helped on a periodic basis and to avoid those few individuals who may take unfair advantage of the aid. Church workers make it clear that assistance is help on a temporary, and not permanent, basis. Records are kept on every person who receives food or clothes or both.

For many of the Christian workers this has been an eye-opening experience. Some were totally unaware that there existed, in the same city and country, people so bereft of much-needed basic sustenance. Through the experience of sharing in this Christian ministry, church members personally experienced the joy that comes from applying the teaching of our Lord when He said:

> Then the King will say to those at his right hand, "Come, O blessed of my Father, inherit the kingdom prepared for you from the foundation of the world; for I was hungry and you gave me food, I was thirsty and you gave me drink, I was a stranger and you welcomed me, I was naked and you clothed me, I was sick and you visited me" (Matt. 25:34-36, RSV)

In recent years a mysterious and difficult-to-diagnose illness has begun to appear in our vast land of plenty. Some famous people, and others not so famous, have contracted this dread malady and died, while others have been able to start on the road to recovery. Medical science is not fully clear as to all the causes for this life-sapping demon. It has been named anorexia nervosa. Victims of this deadly disease are convinced they are too fat and need to stop eating and should take diet pills or laxatives to deflate their imagined overweight condition. Little by little some of these poor individuals waste away and die, despite everything that is done—psychiatric care, special nutritional diets, or intravenous nourishment.

It is ironic. In the midst of plenty, young women waste away because they think they are too fat, and other people suffer because they are hungry but cannot obtain sufficient food. Could it be we are experiencing the rewards of self-indulgence, gluttony, indifference to human need, and spiritual famine?

The debauchery of ancient Rome was ugly, but it seems proper to compare that profligate society to the United States. Recorded history shows that when Rome was at its peak of disgusting wastefulness and godlessness that some rich and powerful citizens would gorge with food, gag themselves so they could vomit, and then eat more. This continued while thousands of Romans went hungry for lack of food. What a sickening example of the depths of waste and lack of concern for humankind!

Next time you're in a restaurant, notice how

much food is discarded because either the serv-
ings were too big, and could not be eaten, or
were picked over and left by wasteful and
spoiled children and adults. Grocery stores
throw out vegetables and fruit after a period of
time that could be consumed by many hungry
people. Our profit motive is so strong that we
throw away good food rather than risk not sell-
ing it for as high a price as the public will toler-
ate.

Earl Davis has written an excellent book
based on themes from The Lord's Prayer. His
comments on the part, "Give us this day our
daily bread" (Matt. 6:11), are thought provoking.
He offers some questions followed by a lovely
illustration from the story of Lazarus.

> For whom am I responsible? What is meant by
> these plural pronouns in the Model Prayer? This *us*
> and *our* bread? Let me stress that when God gives
> bread to one, he gives bread to all. God intends that
> we share. That is surely the thrust of the story of
> Lazarus and Dives. . . . You remember that at the end
> of the story Lazarus went to heaven and the rich man
> went to hell. But it is pure speculation to say the rich
> man was obviously an evil man. No, the truth of the
> matter is the rich man's sin was simply this, he was
> content and complacent while his fellowman lived in
> poverty, need, and hopelessness!
> God makes enough bread for everybody to eat;

the problem is that so often you and I do not share the bread.[2]

Someone has estimated that if every church of every denomination would take care of the total needs—food, housing, clothing, medicine, and employment—of three poor families that government welfare would not be needed. What a sad commentary on our thousands of churches! We have buildings, resources, and personnel to respond to human need, and yet the percentage of benevolence is low compared to the actual needs literally screaming for attention. God forgive us!

Most of my childhood and teen years were spent in the so-called "Bible Belt." Carefully follow my thoughts as they are presented. What I am about to offer is not a full-scale challenge for churches to sell out to social ministry. That has been the error of major denominations at times, and it would be wrong for any church or group of churches to focus their main attention in such endeavors. It seems to me, however, that it is equally possible for a church, churches, or a denomination to devote an inordinate amount of personnel and monies to evangelism alone and neglect human physical need. Read me correctly and recall Jesus' teachings to learn that the people of God must seek to meet both the spiritual and physical needs of the humanity He has created.

No wonder our outreach to mankind is not as rapid as it should and can be. Too often our evangelism is suspect because we shout about the love of God and our love and then fail to express that love in a concrete, substantial manner. It is my strong conviction that immeasurably more would walk the aisles of our churches on Sundays and Wednesdays if the people of God would aggressively and practically seek to meet human physical needs. It is hard to hear John 3:16 when your stomach is aching with hunger pangs and your children are shivering from the cold due to lack of warm clothes. One reason we do not reach these kinds of people could be: even if they did eventually come to our churches they would be out of place anyway. Again, God forgive us!

Many of us can recall thousands of words on many Sundays in nice churches and humble tent meetings that proclaimed the glorious appeal for sinful, wretched people to be saved. Yet, the verbage appealing to Christians to meet human physical needs were miniscule in number and heard primarily during the Thanksgiving or Christmas seasons. Look at the budgets of most churches. The percentage spent on ourselves is blazingly evident in comparison to allocations for others.

On a national scale our preoccupation with arms is far surpassing our concern with the meeting of world hunger. In 16 hours the U.S. military spends more than the World Health and the Food and Agriculture Organization spend a year. Reread Matthew 25:34-36 and then read verses 37-46 for even stronger words from our Lord about meeting human needs.

Hymn writer William J. Reynolds vividly portrays Scriptural teaching about consistency in meeting both physical and spiritual needs:

How do you share the love of Jesus with a lonely man?
How do you tell a hungry man about the Bread of Life?
How do you tell a thirsty man about the Living Water of the Lord?

How do you tell a dying man about eternal life?
How do you tell an orphan child about the Father's love?
How do you tell a man who's poor about the wondrous riches of the Lord?

How do you tell a loveless world that God himself is love?
How do you help a man who's down to lift his eyes above?
How do you tell a bleeding man about the healing power of the Lord?

How do you tell him of his Word?
People who know go to people who need to know
    Jesus;
People who love go to people alone without Jesus;
For there are people who need to see,
    people who need to love,
    people who need to know God's redeeming love.
People who see go to those who are blind without
    Jesus,
And this is people to people, yes,
    people to people,
All sharing together God's love.[3]

Both at home and abroad the people of God need to redouble their efforts in telling the good news of His love for all people, while at the same time showing them the generous expressions of love that flow from those committed to Him. It is a gargantuan task. It is easy to be overcome by the immensity of reaching the world for Christ if we forget, "For he who is in you is greater than he who is in the world" (1 John 4:4 b, RSV). Author Richard Bach expressed it aptly: "Argue for your limitations and sure enough, they're yours."[4]

6
Manna Through the Bakery Window

The first part of my childhood was spent in the cold North of Fort Wayne, Indiana. When I say cold I mean wintertime temperatures way below zero, snow, and biting winds. In the 1930s my Southern-bred parents left a struggling existence in the rural South. Father was able to locate employment in Indiana away from more moderate temperatures. But the people were warm-natured and the job was good, so off to the North my parents traveled. They knew the blessings of honest work, good friends, and a vibrant church in their new setting.

I had the privilege of being born into this environment. As time went on my world expanded to include several friends outside home. Speaking of friends, they are a blessing at any age level in life. One of my best friends had an aunt who worked in a bakery in the next block. She never married and she enjoyed spoiling children, especially my friend and me. I don't recall when the tradition began, but this aunt and we two youngsters had a binding agreement that stood as long as she worked at the bakery. Whenever hunger pangs struck our boyish systems, help was not far away. A short run down the alley to the bakery was a frequent answer to our food supply dilemma. In the alley behind the bakery was a stack of bricks against the outside wall. The bricks were conveniently located directly beneath a window, and one windowpane had a large hole in it. This set of circumstances made it possible for a miraculous happening for two hungry chaps!

After my friend and I would climb atop the brick pile one of us would shout through the hole in the window, "Mabel, Mabel!" Her work station was close enough to the window so she could hear our mournful pleas. Soon after we called her, an amazing thing began to happen. Fresh, hot, jelly-filled doughnuts would begin squeezing through the hole in the window. Imagine the eager hands of two boys accepting this "manna" through the bakery window. In the wilderness of our need came blessings from one who loved us.

That was long ago, and even now when I

pass a bakery or doughnut shop I fondly remember that hole in the bakery window. Your needs and mine are met in many obvious ways and through others not quite as obvious.

Through the years I have complained too often for lack of something or other. How about you? Like thousands of fellow American believers in this half of the twentieth century I forget to acknowledge many blessings of God. These blessings are all around and within us. For us to realize the existence of these blessings we need to stop, think, and notice them. One of my favorite old hymns catches the sentiment of the value of recognizing blessings:

> When upon life's billows you are tempest tossed,
> When you are discouraged, thinking all is lost,
> Count your many blessings, name them one by one,
> And it will surprise you what the Lord hath done.
>
> Are you ever burdened with a load of care?
> Does the cross seem heavy you are called to bear?
> Count your many blessings, ev'ry doubt will fly,
> And you will be singing as the days go by.
>
> When you look at others with their lands and gold,
> Think that Christ has promised you his wealth untold;
> Count your many blessings, money cannot buy
> Your reward in heaven, nor your home on high.
>
> So, amid the conflict, whether great or small,
> Do not be discouraged, God is over all;

Count your many blessings, angels will attend,
Help and comfort give you to your journey's end.

Count your blessings, name them one by one:
Count your blessings, see what God hath done;
Count your blessings, name them one by one;
Count your many blessings, see what God hath done.
—Johnson Oatman

Too often we are like the people of Israel as recorded in Exodus 16—17. They were out from under the cruel hands of Pharaoh. God was taking care of them providently. One way His care was shown was His provision of manna in the wilderness. Even though their needs were being met, they complained. My mother used this chant on me when as I child I would want this or that:

Always wanting what is not
Never satisfied with what you've got!

This little rhyme accurately describes the ancient people of God, and it also depicts a host of Christ's followers today.

During my adolescent days in Charlotte, North Carolina, I had the pleasure of worshiping in a Southern Baptist church often visited by the father of Evangelist Billy Graham. Mr. Frank was a dedicated Presbyterian farmer and dairyman. He liked to attend our evening worship to hear our pastor preach and to fellowship with acquaintances. Usually he was called on to pray. Never will I forget this saint of God as he poured out his soul to the Heavenly Father.

He would pray for the sick, the unsaved, our church, his church, all of the people of God, his evangelist son, other family members, and more. His talk with God was so real I would open my eyes, peeking to see if I could see God. God was so personal to him that it challenged me to be more aware of the reality and care of God. At the close of the evening service Mr. Frank would slip away, greeting a few as he left. His humble attitude did not allow him to be gloated over as the father of a great evangelist. Mr. Frank was a blessing to me in my youth and to many others.

Blessings of God are all around you and me. In our town there is a learning-deficient woman known affectionately as the "Candy Lady." She looks sort of like a "bag lady" from New York because she wears an old overcoat and carries a big bag. In that bag is a wide assortment of candy. Her delight in life is roaming in and out of the downtown stores and up and down sidewalks giving pieces of hard candy to store clerks and frequently to shoppers. One store clerk told me the Candy Lady is most disappointed if you do not accept the candy, so it's best to receive her gifts.

The Candy Lady has captured the spirit of Christian generosity. There is an innocent sweetness in her distribution of friendliness and sweet treats. Verses of Scripture come to mind as I think of this person: "Let brotherly love continue. Do not neglect to show hospitality to strangers, for thereby some have entertained angels unawares" (Heb. 13:1-2, RSV).

I don't know if the Candy Lady is an angel, but then again I don't know if she is not. It is clear to me that few Christians spread as much love and sunshine as the Candy Lady.

Surely our Lord is disappointed when He offers so many blessings and we ignore them, do not accept them, or are not even aware of them.

Carl Bates shares a personal experience that beautifully illustrates the blessings of God and how we miss out on them. Following a pastorate in Florida in the 1940s Dr. Bates was called as pastor of a large Texas Baptist church. His first Sunday there he preached the gospel the best he could in his seersucker suit. Following the worship service he was greeting people as they left the sanctuary. One rather ordinary fellow came through the line of worshipers and said, "Dr. Bates, we enjoyed your sermon this morning. We want our pastor to make a good impression in the community. I have made arrangements at a local clothing store for you to select a complete wardrobe this week." With this, he disappeared into the crowd.

Naturally, Dr. Bates was anxious to visit the clothing store as soon as possible. Not wishing to overtax the bank account of this ordinary-looking church member he selected a suit, shirts, ties, shoes, and a belt that were good, but not the top quality, expensive merchandise the store had to offer. The clerk kept asking Dr. Bates, "Are you sure this is all you wanted." He assured the clerk of his satisfaction and they loaded the new purchases in his car.

Later that week Bates learned that the ordinary fellow who sponsored the wardrobe was worth many millions of dollars. He had underestimated the resources of his benefactor and deprived himself of much more. This is how disciples of the living Lord do many times. They underestimate the resources of the mighty King of kings and Lord of lords and miss out on many of His rich blessings.

Blessings from God are all around us. If only we could avoid thoughts that obstruct our view. A preschool girl in my church gives me a hug and chatters happily to me each Wednesday during the church dinner. Her innocent expression of affection reminds me of our children when they were young. It feels good to be loved.

Honest, pure love shown by this precious child is one of God's blessings on me.

Each month a group of our retired adults and I go visit a local nursing home. The smiles and words of appreciation from the residents give us rewarding blessings. Bringing cheer feels good deep down inside.

A friendly neighborhood cat or dog waiting for a pat on the head or birds warbling their beautiful songs are all part of the blessings of God.

There is constant "manna" from God for those who consciously desire to observe, to taste, and to enjoy. The followers of Christ can receive the blessings of God and not even know it. Or they can live in an attitude of thankfulness to God so they can recognize the bounty of God in thousands of ways.

Dear Father of all manna,
Manna is all around and in me because of your great love.
Anticipation for what you can do through me is needed.
Nothing can keep you from loving me or anybody.
Noticing your love is up to me.
Accept my love for you and generate in me a new awareness of the possibilities for me to be a blessing to others.
In Jesus' Name.
Amen.

7

Oranges Come from Trees

"Praise God from whom all blessings flow." It may sound trite, but we have innumerable blessings for which to be grateful. Like the old hymn, "Count Your Many Blessings," reminds us, we need to "name them one by one." Sometimes we thank God for the whole world rather than specific objects we see in that lovely world. This is kind of like the saying, "Sometimes you can't see the trees for the forest."

Many gifts come to us in boxes or packages like presents at Christmastime, colorful and bright under Christmas trees, or birthday presents on the dining room table beside a cake with candles. For parents on Father's Day or Mother's Day it is not always the gifts in boxes that have the deepest meaning. On these days it is thrilling to have children send handmade or carefully selected cards or, even better, to hear on the telephone or in person words like, "Hey, Dad (or Mom), I love you!" However these kinds of presents come, and in whatever form, they are precious gifts. They help us to be thankful to God, if we let them.

Far more blessings come from God than in man-made containers. In many hymnals is the joyful hymn, "This Is My Father's World." The words by Maltbie D. Babcock remind us of many blessings which cause our hearts to sing and our lips to speak words of rejoicing. Read them carefully.

> This is my Father's world,
> And to my list'ning ears,
> All nature sings, and round me rings
> The music of the spheres.
>
> This is my Father's world,
> I rest me in the thought
> Of rocks and trees, of skies and seas;
> His hand the wonders wrought.
>
> This is my Father's world,
> The birds their carols raise;
> The morning light, the lily white
> Declare their Maker's praise.
> This is my Father's world,
> He shines in all that's fair;
> In the rustling grass I hear him pass,
> He speaks to me ev'rywhere.

This is my Father's world,
O let me ne'er forget
That though the wrong seems oft so strong,
God is the Ruler yet.
This is my Father's world,
The battle is not done;
Jesus who died shall be satisfied,
And earth and heaven be one."

Many selections written by the psalmist indicate praise to God for blessings in nature. The first stanza of Psalm 19 is one of numerous examples: "The heavens declare the glory of God; and the firmament sheweth his handiwork."

How often we take things for granted. A few years ago a cousin and aunt of mine told me about their childhood dream which came true. Both of these women were born in the country, Spartanburg County, South Carolina. At Thanksgiving and Christmas it was a tasty treat for them to receive an apple, an orange, or maybe some stick candy. Times were hard, but there was an abundance of family love and appreciation for even the simplest of gifts.

In this country setting with red clay, hot summers, colorful falls, and bitter winters, there were many kinds of trees. Apple trees provided fruit for making pies and cobblers. I can almost smell those fresh-apple desserts right now. My relatives also looked forward to the harvesting of juicy, tree-ripened peaches. From the peaches came tasty additions of cereal and milk, or they were sliced with a well-worn "Old Timer" or "Case" pocket knife and eaten under the shade of an old oak tree. Other peaches were turned into cobblers or pies or canned for later use.

Apple, peach, and fig trees were familiar to the people who lived on farms. But one kind most people had never seen was an orange tree. My cousin and aunt had enjoyed oranges maybe twice a year, but they had never seen oranges growing on trees.

After many years on the farm and in cotton mills, these dear ladies retired. They had looked forward to going places they had never been and seeing things they had never seen, except in magazines, movies, or television. They had always wanted to visit Florida to see oranges actually growing on trees. Finally, they got together with other family members and drove down to Florida. When they approached the first orange grove they stopped the car. The grove owner gave them permission to look at the oranges and to pick a few. There must have been basic communication between these South Carolina and Florida farmers. Years of planting and harvesting brought them in touch with the marvels of the Creator's handiwork.

My relatives told me they acted like children in that Florida orange grove. They were at long last able to see in person the trees from which came the oranges they had delighted in as humble country folk in South Carolina. Because of a strong Christian heritage this aunt and cousin said they thanked God for oranges and the health, even in old age, enabling them to travel to see oranges growing on trees.

I told this story during a sermon delivered at a community Thanksgiving service. It was amazing to hear other people, after the service that day, tell about some personal experiences or about relatives who had also cherished God's bountiful world. One lady shared this with me. After her mother died they discovered in a cabinet an old, dusty album. In that album was a flat, dried orange. Somewhere along the way a child of God had marveled at the beauty of an orange and had included it in a collection of memories.

Isn't it refreshing to know there are still people who can be thrilled over small blessings like oranges? In America we have plenty for which to be thankful: freedom of speech; civil law and order; an extensive highway system for convenience of pleasure travel and commerce; peace, which is a complex and fragile commodity; "snowflakes that cling to my nose and eyelashes"; a car that starts in winter; a store clerk who smiles whether or not you buy anything; lab experiments that work out; children laughing; warm houses in winter, ad infinitum.

We should be thankful. And we need to be serious in our thinking when we hear statistics to the effect that perhaps sixteen to seventeen million children die each year from malnutrition and related causes. In our country alone there is enough food thrown away to feed these hungry children, and probably their mothers and fathers.

An *attitude of gratitude* is essential to the emotional health of individuals, families, and nations. Gratitude lifts one from self. It causes one to recognize the need for others and the needs of others. It aids in the restoration of relationships between mankind and the Redeemer God.

A great contemporary preacher and theologian, Fred Craddock,[1] wrote a poem, "The Main Thing," for an offspring graduating from college. The provocative poem asks the question, "What is the main thing?" After many years of family support, associations with teachers or other friends, and certain exposure to the realities of life, the child, Craddock hoped, would know the answer to the question. But he was disappointed. According to this godly father the main thing is "gratitude."

You may have heard the story of the family on a picnic. One of the children ventured too far into a nearby lake to wade. He fell into deep water and began to drown. Nobody in the family knew how to swim. They were petrified with terror. A stranger came by, saw the situation, dived into the water, clothes and all; saved the child, and brought him back to the anxious, waiting arms of his mother. Instead of eager words of gratitude she blurted out, "He had a cap on. Where is his cap?"

In the George Bernard Shaw play *Arms and the Man,* Act III, Bluntschli and Raina are having a conversation. Bluntschli at one point asks, "Do you like gratitude? I don't. If pity is akin to love, gratitude is akin to the other thing." Raina responds, "Gratitude: If you are incapable of gratitude you are incapable of any noble sentiment. Even animals are grateful."[2] The words of this fictional character have the ring of truth to them. If you have ever come in contact with a truly ungrateful human being, you can attest to this fact: that person is selfish and basically unhappy.

The writer of Psalm 67 was keenly aware of mankind's dependence on God to grant the harvest for food. The psalmist went beyond the seasonal reaping to express the conviction of the ultimate purpose God has for all nations. Ancient Israel believed God was the source of all blessings. As we are grateful to God we avoid an

incessant focus on who we are and what we see
with the naked eye. God would have His followers look at spiritual aspects as most important,
but He would also have us look at earthly things
and be reminded of heavenly truths. Just as sure
as wheat seeds must die before they can grow
more wheat, so must you and I die to self in order
to grow more like our Master. There is always
the promise of harvest, yet we must always remember that God is the harvester, not us.

In a sense both the arms race hawks and the
pacifists may risk an impertinent attitude toward
God and His ultimate purpose if they are not
careful. But, then, the vast noninvolved majority
between these two poles risk experiencing tyr-
anny sowed by godless governments. Neither
preparation for obliterating the enemy nor pas-
sively waiting to be blotted out seem satisfactory
solutions. Hence, whatever decisions are made
should never be dependent exclusively on even
the best of political scientists. We desperately
need to turn to God for guidance in decision-
making. He is our only hope!

The apostle Paul teaches in Philippians 4
basically this: As we think mercy we will be mer-
ciful. As we think truth we will be truthful. As we
think peace we will be peace makers. As we
think gratitude we will be grateful. As we think
love we will love God and fellowman. As we

think trust in God for all of the needs of life, we will be supplied. When the thoughts of mankind are pure, the search for peace, purpose, and praise to God is productive and satisfying.

On the radio I heard a funny, but also pitifully true, story about atheists. A group of atheists had joined hands around a Thanksgiving table. They said, "Thank you, Paine-Webber." It is sad when people think of thankfulness for success as being something they alone did or they and their Wall Street investments did. A rigid, self-sufficient attitude robs mankind of a right relationship with God and man. An attitude of thankfulness toward God for earthly life and eternal life is the key to appreciating the fact that oranges come from trees.

Joyce Kilmer expresses conviction and gratitude this way:

I think that I shall never see
A poem lovely as a tree.

A tree whose hungry mouth is prest
Against the earth's sweet flowing breast;

A tree that looks at God all day
And lifts her leafy arms to pray;

A tree that may in Summer wear
A nest of robins in her hair;

Upon whose bosom snow has lain;
Who intimately lives with rain.

Poems are made by fools like me,
But only God can make a tree.

The first time I saw oranges growing on trees the scene appeared almost unreal. It was probably the newness of the tropical climate and different vegetation that helped me feel that way about the oranges. Where I had lived most of my life there was the changing of seasons. The plants and trees of my childhood setting were unlike those in a warmer climate. After vacationing in Florida for a while the trees and plants there became less unusual. Isn't it interesting how we can adapt to things around and within us? At times we adjust so well that our new locale no longer seems attractive or unusual.

Getting used to our surroundings is good in some ways. It is sad if we become so used to our surroundings that we fail to notice little things and new additions. Prayers of thanksgiving at meals can become a routine if we are not careful. Forgetting the marvelous grace of God in our lives stunts our spiritual vitality, leading to boredom in service. Instead of bearing fruit we become ornamental and artificial like man-made Christmas trees that are stored, only to be brought out when it is convenient for the season.

Oranges come from trees, real trees. Real trees come from God.

Oh Dear Heavenly Father,
Thank you for oranges and
    all your other blessings.
Teach us the joy of thankful
    hearts and voices.
May we be like trees planted
    by rivers of water and be fruitful
    servants.
In the Name of Christ our Creator
    and Harvester we pray.
    Amen.

8
Solid Food that Lasts

When a hardworking person has finished his labors a solid meat-and-potatoes-type meal is far more satisfying than a snack. On interstate highways there are signs reading like, "Get a truck driver's meal" or "Working man's lunch served." In many cities across the country there are restaurants known for serving solid meals, large in quantity and high in protein, a stick-to-your-ribs fare.

One way I, a city-slicker boy with a country flair, made money was cutting grass and plowing gardens. No doubt I was influenced by my country-bred parents and relatives. It wasn't a mule or horse team that pulled my plow, but what I plowed with bucked as much or more! That old gas engine drove a garden tiller, and when I hit hard ground, small stumps, roots, or rock, it would knock me for a loop! There was never a lack of work in that large North Carolina city. For one thing people were glad to have somebody else do the work. Another reason was I was about the only kid who would do that sort of work. Besides that, I worked for low wages, $1 to $1.50 an hour. That was low even for the 1950s.

Mother knew I needed solid food before I left early in the morning so she prepared a hefty breakfast. If I needed a lunch packed she would put in extra appetizers—apple, banana, raisins, a candy bar—along with a couple of "Dagwood" sandwiches. When I came home from a long day of plowing and grass-cutting my taste buds screamed for more than a bowl of soup and a stalk of celery. She knew I needed solid food that lasts, that alleviates hunger, and gives energy.

When we followers of Christ recall the last Passover our Lord celebrated with the twelve disciples, our attention is given to the juice and bread. Christians know that these two elements became reminders of the sacrifice Christ made on the cross. The fruit of the vine reminds us of the atoning blood He shed for the sins of mankind. The bread reminds us of His body that was abused, nailed to a cruel cross, buried, and then brought back to life by the power of God.

Before the cup and bread were served at

the Passover meal a solid feast was enjoyed by all the disciples.

> At the Passover in the time of Christ, observed officially at Jerusalem, the paschal lambs were slain in various sections of the capital and taken to the priests to have their sacrificial portions presented at the altar. The remaining portions of the lambs were then taken to the houses, where no fewer than 10 men and not more than 20 ate one animal, like Christ and his 12 disciples.[1]

The description goes on to include bitter herbs, which reminded the Jews of the bitterness of Egyptian bondage, unleavened cakes dipped in a sweet sauce, and more, all of which reveal that a solid meal was enjoyed by the disciples before Christ gave them and us new symbols.

The Passover or Seder meal still reminds Jewish worshipers of one act of God in the past. The Lord's Supper reminds Christians of an act of God in the past and that it has continuous power through eternity. In Christ there is a solid foundation for life now and forevermore. Like solid food which is filling and lasting, so is the solid food of the Spirit of the Living God.

Edward Mote expressed confidence in the saving Lord when he wrote the beautiful words of "The Solid Rock" which were set to music by William Bradbury:

My hope is built on nothing less
Than Jesus' blood and righteousness;
I dare not trust the sweetest frame,
But wholly lean on Jesus' name.

When darkness seems to hide his face,
I rest on his unchanging grace;
In ev'ry high and stormy gale,
My anchor holds within the veil.

His oath, his covenant, his blood
Support me in the whelming flood;
When all around my soul gives way,
He then is all my hope and stay.

When he shall come with trumpet sound,
Oh, may I then in him be found;
Dressed in his righteousness alone,
Faultless to stand before the throne.

On Christ the solid Rock, I stand;
All other ground is sinking sand,
All other ground is sinking sand.

Mote said he wanted to write a hymn on the "Gracious experience of a Christian." The day he wrote the hymn he saw a friend whose wife was seriously ill. His friend carried the words of the first two verses to his sick wife so she could enjoy them. The words encouraged her considerably. Her husband told Mote about the positive reaction later that day, and he wrote two additional verses which he delivered to his dear Christian friends.[2] In the face of death the reminder of the solid rock, Christ Jesus, brought joy, courage, and comfort to the first reader of that great hymn.

Mankind still persists in placing confidence in types of security residing in possessions, military power, and knowledge. These kinds of security are temporary. As magnificent as the Biltmore mansion is, it is a prestigious museum for tourists, no longer a home for elegant, wealthy people. Great men of knowledge in the past have made contributions to this world, yes, but many of their concepts are out of date or have the potential of being replaced. Valiant men with good or bad intentions have marched across states, countries, and continents, and they, too, are either remembered in history books, legends, and statues, or are completely forgotten.

As the apostle Paul wrote, "Love never ceases." It is comforting to know that Christ, the source of eternal love, reigns eternally. A friend of mine related an experience he had during World War II. It is an unusual episode revealing the foolishness of war and the common ground of communication possibility when people love God and one another and respect the eternal values found only in the truth of the Word of God.

The eighteen-year-old German was in a small group of POWs in an American-controlled camp in France. The American soldier guarding the camp was a quiet, gracious East Tennessee country farmer. Both men were victims of a war they did not start, but, because of respective national duty, were active participants.

Friendship developed between the Yankee and Nazi. Special favors in the form of food rations and candy bars came to be regular treats from the victor to the foe. When the German requested juice and a cross and bread for communion, the Tennessee farm boy gladly responded. Amid cruel war, worship of God was needed by everyone, whether in Europe or the United States.

In this atmosphere it was no longer conqueror and defeated, right or wrong. A strong desire for an end to military struggle, hopes of returning home to pick up life and the pursuit of happiness, and the reaching for personal goals were uppermost in the minds of both the guard and the prisoner. The young German shared with the American GI his ambition to attend medical school for training as a physician. After the war was over the American wished to return home to his new wife and begin business as a florist. Isn't it compelling how both men had thoughts of healing and beauty despite the presence of hurt and destruction?

Finally World War II ended, and winners

and losers made their way back to their home-
lands. Years passed and the booming 1950s
came. The American and his wife were success-
ful in the florist shop in a small town nestled in
the shadow of the Great Smoky Mountains. Hos-
pitalization became necessary for the businessman. One day while lying in a Baptist medical
center, this former military prison guard heard
a familiar name on the hospital intercom.

The doctor being paged had a familiar German name. Could it be the same fellow who had
once been a prisoner and had dreams of being a
doctor? After a nurse was buzzed and inquiries
made, there came a reunion of two men who had
years earlier been thousands of miles away from
this place, waging war. What a difference. Instead of the main goal of inflicting pain and
securing confinement, there now was a mutual
concern for discovering healing and nurturing
freedom. A few years earlier food rations and
candy came from the American to the German
in prison surroundings. Now medical care came
from the German to the American in an atmosphere of freedom, love, and security.

John 8:36 comes to mind. Jesus declared,
"So if the Son makes you free, you will be free
indeed"(RSV). Somewhere earlier in their lives
the two men of our story had each tasted the
secure, solid food that lasts. When they came in

contact with each other in France and Tennessee the strength of their spiritual diet was such that they could relate to each other on a plane impossible outside of Christ. This mutual plane of security is not established by human sight or human power or human possessions or human knowledge. It is based on the solid food that lasts and is discovered through faith in the Eternal God.

Poet and hymnwriter Daniel W. Whittle expresses mature faith in Christ in his hymn, "I Know Whom I Have Believed":

I Know not why God's wondrous grace
To me he hath made known,
Nor why, unworthy, Christ in love
Redeemed me for his own.

I know not how this saving faith
To me he did impart,
Nor how believing in his Word
Wrought peace within my heart.

I know not how the Spirit moves,
Convincing men of sin,
Revealing Jesus thro' the Word,
Creating faith in him.

I know not when my Lord may come,
At night or noon-day fair,
Nor if I'll walk the vale with him,
Or meet him in the air.

But I know whom I have believed,
And am persuaded that he is able
To keep that which I've committed
Unto him against that day.

Whittle obviously based much of his thought for this testimony on the words of faith by an ancient man of faith, the apostle Paul: "But I am not ashamed, for I know whom I have believed, and I am sure that he is able to guard until that Day what has been entrusted to me" (2 Tim. 1:12, RSV).

When John Paton, the pioneer missionary to the New Hebrides, was translating the Scriptures into the language of the people of the South Seas, he had difficulty securing a word for faith. There seemed to be no equivalent in the language.

On a hot afternoon, one of Paton's workers came in from a hard day's work. Leaning back on a lounge chair, the man panted, "Oh, I'm so tired, I feel I must lean my whole weight on this chair." "Praise God!" shouted Paton, "I've got my word: God so loved the world that He gave His only begotten Son, that whosoever leaneth his whole weight on Him shall not perish, but have everlasting life."

Emily Dickinson wrote the poem, "Chartless." She hauntingly expresses the essential element of faith in our reach to God:

> I never saw a moor,
> I never saw the sea;
> Yet know I how the heather looks.
> And what a wave must be.
>
> I never spoke with God,
> Nor visited in heaven;
> Yet certain am I of the spot
> As if the chart were given.

9
Eat Something When You Go Back Home

A tradition in many parts of our country following a funeral service is to visit in the home of the bereaved family. This custom usually is reserved for the immediate members of the family, close relatives, and dearest of friends. It is customary at this gathering to enjoy the abundance of food provided by neighbors and church members.

It may appear somewhat indifferent for the family and other guests to partake of a delightful array of foods so soon after a burial service. From another perspective it is sort of a practical recognition that those who are alive must go on, must take nourishment.

For Christians the fear and dread of death can be eased as they recognize that the ending of physical life is not the end at all. The early disciples were troubled with the same concerns about life after death. Through the years mankind has had pressing questions about what is beyond the grave, beyond the last, struggling heartbeat that ushers a soul into eternity. Almost two thousand years ago Jesus left comforting words and hope that extend to disciples of every era.

> Let not your hearts be troubled; believe in God, believe also in me. In my Father's house are many rooms; if it were not so, would I have told you that I go to prepare a place for you? And when I go and prepare a place for you, I will come again and will take you to myself, that where I am you may be also. And you know the way where I am going. Thomas said to him, "Lord, we do not know where you are going; how can we know the way?" Jesus said to him, "I am the way, and the truth, and the life; no one comes to the Father, but by me" (John 14:1-6, RSV).

The increasing threat of nuclear war, the rise in the number of incidents of violence in this country and around the world, and the awareness mankind has of the aging process, all contribute to an intensified emphasis on death. To untold millions, especially youth and young adults, the threat of death before they can achieve their goals seems unjust and unfair. Their feelings seem justified. It is unfair and unjust not to have some hope for success in this life.

For many this ever-present scratching at the door of life by death brings on depression and bitterness.

November 22, 1983, marks the date of the tragic assassination of President John F. Kennedy. Like many Americans who recall that black Friday, my wife and I continue to share with people around the world a deep sense of regret and sadness because of his death. My wife has an added feeling of hurt because she was introduced personally to him when he was a senator running for our nation's highest office. Nadine shook the extended hand of a famous figure who no longer shares in the vitality of national and international strategy. She never dreamed that a few years from that handshake she would be standing on the streets of Washington, D.C., with a husband, a nine-month-old baby girl, and a quiet throng of people observing a horse carrying a pair of empty boots and an empty saddle. We all were shocked and profoundly aware of the reality of life and death.

While we were waiting for the funeral cortege to proceed past us, the sky over the nation's capital was gray and the air bitter cold. Something ironic happened that day that I shall long remember. You will recall the stand for human rights the president, his attorney-general brother Robert, and many other leaders were taking at that period of time. A lovely black woman in the crowd had noticed the uncovered hands of our daughter. She came over to us and said to my little girl in my arms, "Sugar, your hands must be very cold! Let me put my pair of red gloves on your little hands to keep them warm." She placed the gloves on the cold, tiny hands of our little offspring. We, of course, thanked her and she disappeared into the crowd. To this day we do not know who that thoughtful lady was, but we recall a special moment when we were the benefactors of love that overcame prejudice.

After we returned to our apartment in Maryland and had something hot to eat and drink, we discussed the events of the week and the historic, meaningful occurrences of that day. We were sad and concerned, but also found strength in the truths of God's Word and in the comforting presence of the Holy Spirit. At our church we enjoyed reinforcement for our hope, as with fellow Christians, we celebrated the spirit of the words of the apostle Paul, "We know that in everything God works for good with those who love him, who are called according to his purpose" (Rom. 8:28, RSV).

The subject of death and reminders of it disturb and frighten people, even in this day of enlightenment and so-called coolness. Let me

give you an example of how some people react-
ed one time.

A hearse in which I was riding pulled into
the driveway of a home. I had just conducted a
graveside service and was returning to our town
in the hearse. The driver of the hearse was new
on the job and new to the area. I was not familiar
with the roads in that area either. After making
several wrong turns it became obvious that we
were lost.

We decided to stop and ask for directions. It
was in the summertime. The people at the house
where we stopped were out on their front porch.
When they saw the hearse coming up their
driveway they immediately got up from their
chairs and ran into the house. Being of Irish de-
scent I seized upon the occasion for a bit of levi-
ty. I knocked on the screen door, and a woman
came cautiously to that door. As she stood staring
at the strange man in the dark-blue suit, me, I
said, "Ma'am, we're not here to pick up somebody. We're just lost and would appreciate it if
you'd give us some directions."

She breathed a sigh of relief, we both
laughed, and she told us how to get back on the
road home. After I was back in the hearse, the
mortician and I had a big laugh but also a stimu-
lating discussion about the fears and superstitions connected with death experienced by

people to this day. Sadly enough these fears and superstitions plague many disciples of the living Lord!

It may seem curious that following these episodes related to death, comments on Advent would appear seemingly out of nowhere. Oddly enough, Advent, death, life after death, and the Second Coming are tied all together. They address what is real and what is life, the uniqueness of humanity, and the particular attention God gives us. Fred Kendall, III, offers a fine illustration of "Eternal Life Now":

> During the winter a gardener collects seed. If one were to look at the seed it would not appear that life was within the small, seemingly dead shell. There is miraculous life there, however. When one becomes a Christian, it does not appear that any physical change has occurred in that life. Just as God has placed life in seed, eternal life has entered the Christian through the Holy Spirit. When the Christian dies, he will receive the full benefits of this gift of God, just as in the spring, seed will come to life when planted in the earth.[1]

Some traditionally selected passages of Scripture relating to the first Sunday of Advent, a preparation for the celebration of the Incarnation, the birth of Christ, are: Isaiah 2:1-5, Matthew 24:36-44, and Romans 13:11-14. All of these verses deal with the quality of life possible under certain circumstances and the anticipation of the Final Things, the Return in triumph of the risen Christ. In physical terms life must come before death. In spiritual terms death must come before life, that is, death to sin and the old way of life. It is easy to see then why the Creation, the Incarnation as celebrated at Christmas, the Death and Resurrection of Christ as observed at Easter, and the Parousia, the Second Coming, are closely related. They are parts of a mysterious and glorious puzzle planned and being rightly assembled by the Eternal God.

A great theologian of another generation, W. T. Conner, sheds light on the Christian concepts of the quality of life, peace, and the seeming incongruity of love applied that brings intense struggle:

Even zealous Christian men may speak deridingly of what Christianity has done for human society. But in spite of that the world is a much better place in which to live than it was when Jesus was born into it. Woman has been partially liberated, childhood respected and, to some extent, protected, human personality valued more highly; and all this because of Jesus and his saving work. Political, industrial, and national ideals are being slowly, but surely, transformed. It is something that nations will now at least apologize for causing a war and try to shift the responsibility in public opinion on others. Great social evils are slowly being outlawed.

Another thing to keep in mind is that there may be in some respects a development of evil over against the development of the kingdom of God. Evil develops in opposition to the good. The subtlest and most dangerous forms of evil do not appear in the midst of heathen darkness. They appear as angels of light in the midst of gospel blessings. Evil tends to become more subtle and intense where gospel light is greatest."[2]

These insightful words by Dr. Conner should call Christians to remember a warning from the apostle Peter to avoid the twisting of the Scriptures:

You therefore, beloved, knowing this beforehand, beware lest you be carried away with the error of lawless men and lose your own stability. But grow in the grace and knowledge of our Lord and Savior Jesus Christ. To him be the glory both now and to the day of eternity. Amen (2 Peter 3:17-18, RSV).

There are many voices heard on radio and television who declare the "final word" as to the intricate meaning of the Incarnation, the Death, the Resurrection, and the Second Coming of Christ. No wonder so many sincere people are confused. Unfortunately, confusion is not only among believers but within the hearts and minds of many precious souls who are reaching and hungering for the truth! One can listen to the conglomeration of "church voices" and begin to wonder if salvation is by faith in Christ or by logical adherence to somebody's creed or doctrine, as good or noble as these may be. Jesus did not say He was "a" way or "some possible" truth. He said He is "the way, and the truth" and He is "the life" (John 14:6). And all this is a gift when faith in Christ is exhibited, declares the apostle Paul in Ephesians 2:8-10.

Who fully understands why pain and death are part of life? Of course, we should attempt to understand better these facts of our existence. But, try as we may, we will ultimately come to the necessity for individual faith in God for life as it is on earth, and as it is in heaven. God is the Source and on Him we must rely.

People of faith rely on Him for eternal life. It is equally vital that they rely on Him for care at the moment of death, as well as for the Second Coming, the consummation of the age.

Matthew deals with the return of our Lord in a clear explanation. His description is not cluttered with spectacular details. He simply records the matter in the words of Jesus in the last part of chapter 24 of his Gospel. No one on earth knows when Jesus is coming. No one knows all the signs leading up to the last minute before this glorious event.

Jesus clearly teaches that there is a difference between those who are ready for His Second Coming and those who are not prepared. Those ready for His coming are faithful servants of the Lord endeavoring to do the will of God. The will of God is not all that complex, it seems to me. Throughout the Word of God our discovery of His will has to do with the recognition that He is Lord, we must have faith in Him, we must be obedient to Him, and we must respond to human need as it is readily apparent both physically and spiritually. All of this is wrapped up in the extraordinary love of God which is also an undeniable truth within the innermost recesses of the minds of people and the redemptive act at Calvary (See Rom. 1; John 3; Ps. 14:1).

One commentator sums up what Matthew declares as appropriate preparation for the Second Coming of Christ:

> What is clear is the fact of separation and the contrast in fates, determined by readiness for *the coming of the Son of man* and not national or family identity. In Matthew the dual emphasis is expressed in *watch* (v. 42) and *be ready* (v. 44).[3]

A dear cousin of mine recently died after a five-year battle with multiple sclerosis. It is not easy to see and hear a loved one fighting with pain and the impending prospect of death. Her parents are dear Christian people, but they are human beings who love their children. In their love they hurt when flesh of their flesh hurts. Those who grin and claim pain in one's body or the death of those we hold dear is simply the Lord's will and we should not cry do not seem to be facing reality. One can read the Gospel accounts of Jesus' life and readily see that He hurt, grieved, agonized over people. But He did not let all that consume Him. What He did was confront the realities of life and trust the Father in everything!

After the funeral of my cousin, my aunt wrote me a touching letter of Christian faith. You can catch her spirit from a few excerpts of that letter:

> We have a peace that we haven't had before, "Just when I need it most." . . . She made her plans. She knew her race had been won. Her war with pain was over. She was not afraid. She said so. She said she had run out of knots ("tie a knot and hang on"). . . . We have cried for five years and more knowing she was so sick. She was diagnosed in 1978. Now she's free. We're at peace because she's free of pain.

This courageous facing of death came to her from her faith in the promises of God and in the God who makes the promises! And all of this figures in the overall plan of God for the ultimate redemption of those who trust Him. It takes faith to accept the existence of God, the birth of

Christ, the death and resurrection of the Son of God, the place prepared for believers for all eternity, and the Second Coming of Christ. They all mesh together in the plan of God and cannot be separated or deleted.

Once I was riding with a fellow-minister friend. In his truck he had a cassette tape player. We were listening to some taped Christian music and a sermon. Near the end of a tape, strange tones began to come through the sound system. When I asked what the sound was he gave me this explanation. His wife worked for a physician whose practice required that recordings of patient heartbeats be produced. After the tapes had been used, the doctor discarded them. Being a practical sort of person my friend's wife periodically brought discarded tapes home for her husband to use. It was sort of eerie when I realized that those tones were actual recordings of human hearts and that each bleep was evidence of life.

As strange as it was to hear those recorded tones of life, so is it unusual, and even peculiar, to live the life of faith. A patient must trust his doctor to interpret rightly the hearbeats of life. Christian wayfarers must trust their Great Physician to interpret rightly the heartbeats of eternal life. The words of a chorus come to mind as I

think about the value of following the Lord
Christ in faith. We used to sing it in youth
groups, but the words have come to mean more
to me through the years:

> The Lord knows the way through the wilderness,
> All I have to do is follow.
> The Lord knows the way through the wilderness,
> All I have to do is follow.
> Strength for today is mine always
> And all I need for tomorrow.
> The Lord knows the way through the wilderness,
> All I have to do is follow.

This little chorus is simple and yet profound.
Three and a half millennia ago the people of God
wandered in a Middle Eastern wilderness, trust-
ing God as best they knew. There was hardship,
life and death, and in it all God provided manna.
They trusted God, and in their wilderness home
they did eat. Problems ensued when their trust
in God failed, and they complained from a lack
of appreciation for God's miraculous provisions.

The people of God today need to be careful
to trust their blessed Leader in the wilderness of
life. Even when death comes they can avoid despair and when they go back home they can eat
something. Spiritual food is found in the promises of God. Trust in the promises of God and

then you can eat something when you go back home from the seeming death traps of life. Every day is Advent. Every day is resurrection. Every day is nearer to the coming of Christ. Let us rejoice!

10
An Appetite for Life

When our daughter Charlotte and son Mark were home with us in East Tennessee, the evening meal was a sort of negotiating time. Concerns like who would get the car, how much money was needed for a date, how high the volume of a stereo could be set in the house without doing major damage to the foundation, parental Christian values as they applied to peer pressure, and other such "high-level" matters were discussed.

The older our children became, the more important dinner time was because it was about the only occasion during the day when we were all together. The times I was late or seemed eager to leave the table brought criticism from our two young adults. Dinner time had become strategic for a sort of family peace talk, a sibling summit conference with the "major powers."

Life was vital to us then and it still is. As long as the children were with us, there was an ongoing attempt to maintain peace, which is not easy in a contemporary family, Christian or not. Teenagers generally assume that freedom to do what they wish is the ideal, ushering in peace to their "imprisoned" lives. Freedom to do what one wishes is a common malady for teenagers as well as for adults. The practice of Christian tolerance for the views of others, to be patient and kind when others are rude or mean, is often scarce within a family, a nation, the world, and even a church.

Peace at home and abroad is an elusive existence. Rest of mind and soul escapes millions of people, you and me. The promoters of a life full of smiles and sweet talk offer life that sounds good, while in reality implying something not entirely in keeping with Scripture. Pastoral counselors and other professional counselors are often overwhelmed with the number of persons seeking peace. Look within your own life, and you can probably detect a bit of restlessness, an absence of peace, a longing for better days. A complete absence of malice, a no-trouble existence, a heaven on earth is not always, nor has it ever been, possible.

An absence of peace does not characterize a practicing Christian disciple. Before you protest this view it might be wise for you to see what the Bible says about peace. Read Matthew 10:28-34 in the King James Version and then again in the modern translation by Charles B. Williams.

> And fear not them which kill the body, but are not able to kill the soul: but rather fear him which is able to destroy both soul and body in hell. Are not two sparrows sold for a farthing? and one of them shall not fall on the ground without your Father. But the very hairs of your head are all numbered. Fear ye not therefore, ye are of more value than many sparrows. Whoever therefore shall confess me before men, him will I confess also before my Father which is in heaven. But whosoever shall deny me before men, him will I also deny before my Father which is in heaven. Think not that I am come to send peace on earth: I came not to send peace but a sword (KJV).

The teaching of Jesus is clear in this passage. We like the early followers of Jesus tend to let the temporary world become more valuable than the eternal things of the kingdom of God. Many of those who first heard these instructions were looking for an earthly Messiah who would rule an earthly kingdom. We fear earthly or physical enemies, as they did, like Nazis, kamikazes, snipers, communists, and terrorists. But are these the real enemies? Read the same passage again in the Williams translation:

> You must never be afraid of those who kill the body, but cannot kill the soul. But rather you must keep on fearing Him who can destroy both soul and body in the pit. Do not sparrows sell for a cent apiece? And yet not one of them can fall to the ground without your Father's notice. Even the very hairs on your head have all been counted by God. So stop being afraid; you are worth more than many sparrows. Therefore, everyone who will own me before men I will own before my Father in heaven, but anyone who disowns me before men I will disown before my Father in heaven. Do not suppose that I have come to bring peace to the earth. I have not come to bring peace but a sword.

The late Paul Turner, one-time pastor of First Baptist Church, Clinton, Tennessee, experienced literal war when he stood for the rights of American blacks back in the 1960s. Friends of his related how at one time during the height of the conflict that a local citizen threw Turner against the trunk of a car and beat him mercilessly. Mr. Turner was a peace-loving man. Why would anybody wish to hurt him? You might comment, "God loves everybody. All Turner was doing was pointing people to the love of God and urging them to show love to blacks. Why would anyone want to abuse a man like that?" It is ironic that today a beloved resident of this same area is famous author Alex Haley, a black American.

In the Matthew passage Jesus is teaching all disciples what they need to hear in every generation until He sees fit to return. Jesus gives us new definitions for what is priceless. He takes His concepts of time and helps us view it from the point of view of eternity. We, like the early disciples, are so caught up in the here and now that our view of eternity is extremely limited. We think of birth, rebirth in Christ, and death. Our understanding of eternity, heaven, beyond the physical grave is tiny compared to how God looks at time.

Lest you say in your mind, *Why, I know all this! What value is it to me to bother reviewing what I already know?* Think with me awhile about evidences of our talk about confidence in eternity and our expressions of doubt. At the death of a friend or loved one I have often seen people of faith seemingly give up, drop out of church, or in other ways exhibit lives of hopelessness. At the point of challenge to give a bona fide Christian response to evil actions or intentions in society (i.e. dishonest business practices, cruelty to humanity on the part of government, unequal hearing in the court system) we are too often quiet or even totally silent. There is also the great reluctance by many Christians to speak openly about their personal relationship with Christ.

There seem to be two unproductive extremes when one views eternity and circumstances as they appear in any given period of history. One extreme is to see everything that happens in our land, Russia, or the Mideast as absolutely a sign from God or a sign of "the last days." The other extreme is not to view the predicaments of mankind and nations as signs of punishment for spiritual rebellion or the results of evil forces working themselves out visibly.

If we believe that God is love and that He intends for people to live in peace, then we must avoid shortsighted answers to long-range questions that may require a long time to answer, if ever. The walls that divide mankind from each other and God are numerous and great. William Hull, theologian and pastor, reminds us of significant matters: "Jesus was the implacable foe of every kind of wall that divided mankind into hostile camps, thereby raising barriers to oneness with each other and with God. But he was the architect of walls that united mankind in peace and provided them equal access to the Father in one Spirit" (Reference to Eph. 2:18).[1]

The peace the apostle Paul refers to is not attained at a negotiation conference by world leaders. This peace is only discovered through faith in the Son of God. Peace from God is in existence in the midst of personal strife or even world war. Dietrich Bonhoeffer knew about this God-originated peace right in the middle of a godless Nazi regime. He could have remained in peaceful surroundings on the seminary campus in New York where he had recently been appointed to the faculty in 1939. But, fellow believers in Germany, his native land, were not living in peace. It was not popular to stand for Christian principles that demanded human dignity and government whose motivation came from an attitude of peace rather than vicious force. So he returned to Germany with courage and resolve and with intentions of peace. But he died at Flossenbürg, April 9, 1945, at the hands of men bent on power, human waste, and senseless crime.[2]

God has been seeking in His own mysterious ways to nudge mankind toward peaceful existence since the dawn of time. A careful study of secular human history shows that peace is a shortlived event. The written Word of God, that we are aware of, shows that short episodes of peace and even then the threats of violence both from within and without the people of God, were always present. The same is true to this day.

My wife and I were born in 1939. Within the years since our births there has been World War II, the Korean conflict, Vietnam, the Cuban Missile Crisis, the assassination of an American president and his brother the attorney general, the assassination of an Egyptian president, the holding hostage of Americans in Iran, the countless known and unknown political murders in the Soviet Union, ad nauseum. In the years since my parents brought me into the world, that world has been in turmoil. Where is peace? Must we always fight and kill in order to be assured of a little peace?

C. S. Lewis spoke volumes when he wrote:

> Human life has always been lived on the edge of a precipice. Human culture has always had to exist under the shadow of something infinitely more important than itself. If men had postponed the search for knowledge and beauty until they were secure, the search would never have begun. We are mistaken when we compare war with "normal life." Life has never been normal. . . . Christianity does not simply replace our natural life and substitute a new one; it is rather a new organization which exploits, to its own supernatural ends, these natural materials.[3]

It is not my intention to declare that war is always going to be so we might as well go at it tooth and nail. Neither is it my position that Christians are to sit idly back and do nothing at all in support of peaceful endeavors. What is important, it seems to me, is for us to be more firmly fixed on our purpose as prescribed by Jesus when He teaches us, "But seek ye first the kingdom of God, and his righteousness; and all these things shall be added unto you" (Matt. 6:33). Look into your own life or into the clearly apparent goals of many churches today, and too often their intentions only vaguely resemble kingdom of God pursuits.

Maybe your Christian life has become more like mine, more like a wayfarer than a pilgrim. For years I have spoken of my Christian experience as that of a wandering pilgrim. I have changed the view of my life as a pilgrim to that of a wayfarer. This change in terminology came about when I heard the late Baptist thinker, Carlyle Marney, describe a pilgrim as one who makes some provisions for his journey. The pilgrim, observed Marney, carries a backpack with him and knows where he is going, whereas the wayfarer just lives off the land, doesn't know where he is going, and lives by faith.

My denomination and other evangelical denominations speak much about faith, but our practice of faith is quite different. It seems we want to arrange the situation as we see it before we think God can act. Our beloved denomination, if it is not careful, will seek peace and other blessings in its own way rather than through an emphasis on faith. Biblical teaching reveals a faith based on trust and love rather than revealed information and forceful strategies.

There is a war being waged. However, this war to which I refer and the Bible clearly instructs, is not primarily fought on gunpowder-dusted fields or continents melted by nuclear fallout. True spiritual warfare is sometimes reflected in and hammered out in human existence. Spiritual conflict is not always clear to us. Nevertheless, it is being fought daily.

Oftentimes, some of the most intense battles rage within human hearts, through patient waiting, or during times of careful instruction. Individuals struggling within their deepest being to reject sin and follow Christ experience battles that could be compared to the Napoleonic wars or to Vietnam rice-paddy skirmishes. Parents who wait as patiently as possible for their children to mature, and make wise decisions about careers or marriage partners, endure personal tensions that could be compared to an ancient Philistine attack on Israel or a Teddy Roosevelt charge up San Juan Hill. Compare this to our Heavenly Father as He waits on all of His children to make good decisions, to mature.

The battle for peace is primarily within the hearts of mankind. Rebellious behavior by individuals or groups have roots far more complex than arguments over property or customs. It may not be intellectually impressive to state this, but the root problem of mankind is sin, rebellion against God.

Recently I commented to some friends: "I wonder if I would have become a Christian if I had not been reared in a Christian home." You see, what concerns me is that much of what I have seen in my own life, and in the life of churches, has tended not to point people to Christ but to self and programs. Also, the struggle for power by ministers or groups of persons within churches or denominations is so different from the message of love and humility proclaimed that I believe I would have misgivings about adopting the Christian message. Years ago the evangelist Billy Sunday preached:

> The Church today needs power. It has plenty of wealth, culture and numbers. There is no substitute for the Holy Spirit and you cannot have power without the Holy Spirit. The Holy Spirit is ours by the promise of Christ. To receive him we must give up all sin and walk in the path of righteousness even if it carries us to our graves or across the seas as a missionary. Give up everything the Lord forbids even if it is as important to you as your hand or your eye.[4]

This spiritual power is still needed by the

contemporary Church. We Christians in America are tempted to see our political or military power as a sole means to an end, a God-given advantage to rightfully take over or protect what we think is right or ours, no matter what. Billy Graham wrote, "When anyone has the power to destroy the whole human race in a matter of hours, it becomes a moral issue. The church must speak out."[5]

In his sermon, "To Live by the Sword," Carlyle Marney began, "If a man will live by the sword, or a nation, he surely better wear it. . . . Can a man expect more of life than his fundamental principles have contained? The answer is, 'No!' A man who lives by the sword is limited to what the sword can get him . . . A church can't have both smoothness and relevancy. And a country can't have dominance and loving neighbors."

Glen Stassen, associate professor of Christian Ethics at Southern Baptist Theological Seminary, was a researcher in nuclear physics.

The Brotherhood Commission of the Southern Baptist Convention published his excellent book, *The Journey into Peacemaking.* This book explains "peacemaking" in the Christian context. In chapter 5, "Transforming Initiatives: Personal and Family," is a most provocative study of Romans 12:14-21. Stassen writes:

Howard Rees, my former campus minister, used to say, "I'm tired of hearing what good Christians don't do. What I want to know is, what are you doing while you're not doing what you don't do?" Some will read Romans 12:14-21 and hear a clear teaching that we must never attack an enemy with nuclear weapons. Such an attack would certainly amount to cursing him and being overcome with evil. Nor must we ever repay his nuclear attack with a nuclear counterattack. That would certainly amount to taking revenge into our own hands and returning evil for evil, if anything would. And it would be mutual suicide.

Others might argue, "Yes, but we still need nuclear weapons to deter the enemy from attacking *us.*"

And then a debate will follow. It will be an important debate, and I do not mean to belittle the issues involved. It *might* even lead to someone taking some preventive actions.

But that debate will probably overlook the positive and practical emphasis to which Paul is pointing.

"Be transformed," Paul writes. And in verses 14-21 he points out four positive, transforming initiatives we can take to make peace.

1. Affirm your enemy's valid interests and pray for him. (Matthew 5:44-45, Romans 12:15) . . . .

2. Talk to your brother and seek agreement. (Romans 12:16 and 18, Romans 15:5-9, Matthew 5:23-25) . . . .

3. Associate with the powerless, who need justice. (Romans 12:13 and 16, Matthew 5:42). Clearly this is not merely a negative teaching about *not* doing something. It is a positive initiative to deal with the injustice, the hunger, the violations of human rights, that fall on the powerless and that cause war.

4. Do not seek to return evil for evil. Instead,

start a transforming initiative . . . (Matthew 5:39). This is the spirit of peacemaker groups. We are not called simply to be against war or nuclear weapons. We are called to take positive, transforming initiatives to do something about them. Something practical. Something preventive. Something transforming.[6]

In chapter nine of this same book Stassen applies these four transforming initiatives to the nuclear arms race.

Poet Henry W. Longfellow struggled with the peace problem back in 1863 when he penned the words, "I Heard the Bells on Christmas Day." Our country was in war. The war was not on foreign soil; it was on this continent and among ourselves. Just six months before the writing of this poem more than forty thousand men were killed, wounded, or listed as missing on both sides at the battle of Gettysburg. It is said that a total of 1,340,000 men were engaged in strife in a population which amounted in 1860 to only 31,443,321. And yet in all of this dismal scene one can see in the stanzas an expression of faith as placed in God, not man. This is insight into what constitutes genuine peace.[7]

I heard the bells on Christmas day
Their old familiar carols play,
And wild and sweet the words repeat
Of peace on earth, good-will to men;

And thought how, as the day had come,
The belfries of all Christendom
Had rolled along the unbroken song
Of peace on earth, good-will to men.

And in despair I bowed my head:
"There is no peace on earth," I said;
"For hate is strong, and mocks the song
Of peace on earth, good-will to men."

Then pealed the bells more loud and deep
"God is not dead, nor doth he sleep;
The wrong shall fail, the right prevail,
With peace on earth, good-will to men."

Till, ringing, singing on its way,
The world revolved from night to day,
A voice, a chime, a chant sublime,
Of peace on earth, good-will to men.

Sometimes Americans forget what price their freedoms cost. People in Poland who long for freedom have a song. It is one sung by the Polish Solidarity movement. One of the lines from that song is deeply touching. "Home has not perished as long as we are alive." I wonder, as long as Christians are alive will we seek peace? In our own lives, in our homes, in our churches, in our towns, in our country, and in our world, will we seek peace as long as we live?

We need to be at peace with the Prince of Peace so we can courageously be peacemakers in our day.

Dear Father of Peace and Love,

Forgive us for returning from time to time
  to our old nature of sinful violence in thoughts
  and deeds.
Fix in us spirits of kindness and peacefulness.
Disturb us with your love that knows no end.
Instill within us our rightful minds to be and to
  do that which is gracious and not haughty,
that which is peaceloving and not warlike,
that which is dependent on you and not on ourselves.
Help us to openly proclaim you to all mankind as the
  only source of peace today and on into eternity.
Until the Day when wars shall cease we place our
  hope, our lives, our trust in Thee.
In the Name of the Prince of Peace, Christ Jesus,
  the highest expression of God's love to all mankind,
  we pray.
Amen.

Notes

Chapter 1

1. William Barclay, *The Gospel of John—Volume I* (Philadelphia: Westminster Press, 1956), p. 85.

2. James E. Carter, *Layman's Bible Book Commentary—Volume 18* (Nashville: Broadman Press, 1984), p. 28.

3. Raymond E. Brown, *The Gospel According to John 1-12* (Garden City, New York: Doubleday & Company, Inc., 1966), pp. 103-104.

4. A. M. Hunter, *The Gospel According to John* (Cambridge, England: Cambridge University Press, 1965), pp. 30-31.

Chapter 2

1. Edward F. Murphy, Compiler, *The Crown Treasury of Relevant Quotations* (New York: Crown Publishers, Inc., 1978), p. 294.

2. *The Broadman Bible Commentary, Volume 9* (Nashville: Broadman Press, 1970), p. 373.

3. Mother Teresa of Calcutta, *The Love of Christ* (New York: Harper & Row, 1982), pp. 73-74.

Chapter 3

1. John Gray, *I & II Kings—A Commentary* (Philadelphia: Westminster Press, 1975), p. 125.

2. *The Interpreter's Bible, Volume III* (Nashville: Abingdon Press, 1954), pp. 40-41.

3. *The Broadman Bible Commentary,* (Nashville: Broadman Press, 1970), p. 167.

4. *Daily Devotional Bible Commentary,* Volume I (Nashville: A. J. Holman Co., 1977), p. 301.

5. William Barclay *The Gospel of Matthew, Volume II* (Philadelphia: Westminster Press, 1958), p. 101.

6. *Daily Devotional Bible Commentary, Volume IV* (Nashville: A. J. Holman Co., 1977), p. 69.

7. Ibid.

Chapter 4

1. "Man Writes Book About Near-fatal Shock Experience" by Dan George, Associated Press writer. Published in the *Oak Ridger,* Oak Ridge, Tennessee, July 20, 1984, p. 3.

2. *The Teacher's Bible Commentary,* Edited by H. Franklin Paschall and Herschel H. Hobbs (Nashville: Broadman Press, 1972), p. 693.

3. L. D. Johnson, *Images of Eternity,* Compiled by Marion Johnson (Nashville: Broadman Press, 1984), p. 57.

Chapter 5

1. Arthur Simon, *Bread for the World* (Grand Rapids, MI: Eerdmans Publishing Co., 1975), p. 3.

2. Earl C. Davis, *Forever, Amen.* (Nashville: Broadman Press, 1982), pp. 94-95.

3. "People to People," Words and Music by William J. Reynolds, 1971. ©Copyright 1971 Broadman Press. All rights reserved.

4. Richard Bach, *Illusions: The Adventures of a*

Reluctant Messiah (New York: Dell Publishing Co., Inc., 1977), p. 100.

Chapter 7

1. Dr. Craddock is professor of New Testament and Preaching at Candler School of Theology, Emory University, Atlanta, Georgia.

2. *Speaker's Resources from Contemporary Literature,* Charles L. Wallis, Editor (New York: Harper & Row, 1965), p. 116.

Chapter 8

1. Madeline S. and J. Lane Miller, *Harper's Bible Dictionary* (New York: Harper & Brothers, 1959), p. 528.

2. William J. Reynolds, *Hymns of Our Faith* (Nashville: Broadman Press, 1964), p. 129.

Chapter 9

1. Fred Kendall III in *Adult Life and Work Lesson Annual 1984-1985,* Edited by Reid Keiger (Nashville: Convention Press, 1984), p. 329.

2. W. T. Conner, *Christian Doctrine* (Nashville: Broadman Press, 1937), pp. 302-303.

3. Frank Stagg in "Matthew," *Broadman Bible Commentary, Volume 8* (Nashville: Broadman Press, 1969), p. 222.

Chapter 10

1. William E. Hull, *Beyond the Barriers* (Nashville: Broadman Press, 1981), p. 130.

2. Dallas M. Roark, *Dietrich Bonhoeffer* (Waco: Word Books, 1972), pp. 21-25.

3. C. S. Lewis, *The Weight of Glory and Other Addresses* (New York: Macmillan Co., 1965), pp. 21-22,25.

4. William T. Ellis, *Billy Sunday: The Man and His Message* (Lee T. Myers, 1936), p. 310.

5. A Billy Graham quote included in the brochure, "The Practice of Nuclear Terrorism." Published by Brethren Peace Fellowship, New Windsor, Maryland.

6. Glen Stassen, *The Journey into Peacemaking* (Memphis: Brotherhood Commission, Southern Baptist Convention, 1983), pp. 33-34.

7. H. Augustine Smith, *Lyric Religion: The Romance of Immortal Hymns* (New York: Fleming H. Revell, 1931), pp. 150-151.